Living Out The Called Life

Running God's Race

By
Kurt Litwiller

Edited by Janelle Litwiller and Michael Milligan

FIRST EDITION

ISBN 9780982657416

Library of Congress Control Number: 2010923808

Published by
NewBookPublishing.com, a division of Reliance Media, Inc.
2395 Apopka Blvd., #200, Apopka, FL 32703
NewBookPublishing.com

Printed in the United States of America

Dedication

This book is dedicated first and foremost to my Lord and Savior Jesus Christ. His great love for me is the reason I have any purpose for my life. I am completely His, and willing to live the life He has called me to live. I also dedicate this book to my parents who taught and modeled to me the life that God wanted me to live. And of course I want to dedicate this book to my wonderful wife Janelle. She is my life partner and my best friend. She daily models the life of Christ before me and is a great partner in ministry. Thank you so much for editing this book. May God receive the glory for this book!

Table of Contents

Introduction

As I look around at the church today, it looks very different from the church in the New Testament times. I am not talking about how the early church met in homes and we meet in buildings that are set up specifically for worship, or even how our music style or order of service is different from their worship style. There is something much deeper. I am talking about the behavior of the church. We need to understand that the church, as we call it, is not an actual building—the church is the people. We can keep on adapting the structure of worship to fit the culture in which we live, but we really need to stop adapting the gospel message to make it appealing to our culture.

Many of today's Christians are not living the way that Jesus commanded us to live according to His Holy Word. People are living with the head knowledge that Jesus is God, but that hasn't actually transformed into a change of heart. A person's belief in God has not changed the way they actually live their life. The early church gave us a great example about how to live a transformed life. They lived their lives in a sold out devotion to their Savior, Jesus Christ. They did not make a decision without testing it to see if it was a pleasing act of worship to their God. Can we live with that kind of sold out devotion to Christ?

My desire in the pages that follow is for Christians

to realize the life that they are called to live. The inspiration behind this book comes from Ephesians 4:1, where Paul says, *"As a prisoner for the Lord, then, I urge you, to live a life worthy of the calling you have received."* As believers in Jesus, we have all received a calling to live our lives for him, not for ourselves. We are no longer supposed to drift through life doing whatever we desire to do. God has a purpose and a plan for your life that will glorify Him. In the book of Ephesians, the first three chapters talk about the grace that God has given us in Jesus Christ. It is all about grace and mercy and the deep love of God. But then, there is this transitional verse in Ephesians 4:1. *"...live a life worthy of the calling you have received".* Since you have received this great gift of grace from God, this is how you should live! If we have truly experienced the grace of Jesus, we are called to live lives that reflect that calling.

The Bible many times compares our lives with a race. In a race, the goal is to receive the prize. Not everyone who runs the race wins the prize. In the same way, many people are not running this spiritual race in a way to win the heavenly prize. We know from scripture that many people will not inherit the kingdom of God.[1] There are even people who think they are going to heaven that will not make it. In Matthew 7:21-23 Jesus says, *"Not everyone who says to me, 'Lord, Lord,' will enter the kingdom of heaven, but only he who does the will of my Father who is in heaven. Many will say to me on that day, 'Lord, Lord, did we not prophesy in your name, and in your name drive out demons and perform many miracles?' Then I will tell them plainly, 'I never knew you. Away from me, you evil doers!'"* There are many people, according to this passage, who think that they are going to heaven, but they will not make it. The Christian walk is much more than just saying you are a Christian and it is more than doing a few things for God here and there. The Christian walk is about a heart change. It is developing a relationship with Jesus Christ that says, *"I will be willing to follow you no matter where you lead me."*

Are you running God's race to receive the reward? Or do you run your own race and make your own rules to follow? Take this journey with me. It just may change the way you run the race!

PART 1

Understanding The Race

Be strong and very courageous. Be careful to obey all the law my servant Moses gave you; do not turn from it to the right or to the left, that you may be successful wherever you go. Do not let this Book of the Law depart from your mouth; meditate on it day and night, so that you may be careful to do everything written in it. Then you will be prosperous and successful.
— Joshua 1:7-8

chapter 1

A Race Marked Out For Us

One of the most important things about running a race is to understand the race in which you are running. How frustrating it would be to run the race and then figure out that you didn't understand the objective of the race. You could have run so much better if you had understood the details ahead of time. Can you imagine standing at the starting line and not knowing if you were running the 100 yard dash or if you were running a marathon?

You must understand the race ahead of time, so that you can be a more effective runner. Hebrews 12:1-3 has a lot to say to us about running the race God has given us to run.

> *[1] Therefore, since we are surrounded by such a great cloud of witnesses, let us throw off everything that hinders and the sin that so easily entangles, and let us run with perseverance the race marked out for us. [2] Let us fix our eyes on Jesus, the author and perfecter of our faith, who for the joy set before him endured the cross, scorning its shame, and sat down at the right hand of the throne of God.*

³ Consider him who endured such opposition from sinful men, so that you will not grow weary and lose heart.

Our race is marked out for us.

Verse 1 says, *"Therefore, since we are surrounded by such a great cloud of witnesses, let us throw off everything that hinders and the sin that so easily entangles, and let us run with perseverance the race marked out for us."* The last phrase jumps out at me, "run the race marked out for us." We need to see that we are not to live our lives by our own desires—we can't live however we want to. God has plans for the people who run in His race. He has given us directions in His Word to help us run this race according to the rules, and we have His Holy Spirit to guide us in the right paths we should take. At one point I really struggled with this passage and what it meant. What does it mean that He has the race marked out for us? Psalms 139:16 says, *"... All the days ordained for me where written in your book before one of them came to be."* Does that mean there is no free will? Does that mean that it is marked out for us and we have no choice but to run it? We know that is not the case. We know we have free will because of the fall of man. We are not robots. The Christian race is marked out for us—but it is up to us whether or not we want to follow that path.

> A man talks about being on the cross country team in college. One of their cross country events was on a golf course. The officials for the race would go out ahead, and place flags

on the course to show the runners where they were supposed to run. A certain color indicated "left turn." Another color meant "right turn." Another meant "straight ahead." There was a race marked out for the runners; and if they had any intention of taking home a medal, they had to follow the course marked out for them. They couldn't say, "Boy, this is a six-mile race, but I've only got four miles in me this morning. I'm going to take a short cut. I hope nobody minds." They couldn't look at a particular hill and say, "That hill just looks nasty. I'm not going to tackle that one today. I'll just skip around it and meet up with the other on the other side." They had to run the race marked out for them.[2]

"They had to run the race marked out for them." So it is in this Christian life. The Bible says over and over again that our life is like a race. Let's look at some ways we can get better at running this race.

Sometimes we don't want to follow the course that God has set for us because it is the harder course. In life, we like to

The Christian race is marked out for us—but it is up to us whether or not we want to follow that path.

follow our own desires or our own course, because we can make the race easier by making our own adjustments to the rules of the race. When running the race for the Lord, the first thing we have to do according to this Hebrews 12 passage is to *"throw off everything that hinders and the sin that so easily entangles."* In a race, you notice a runner runs wearing shorts and a tank top. Their clothes are tight so that when they run, they do not get caught up in their attire which slows them down. How much would people laugh at someone who showed up at a race wearing a big winter coat and a big pair of baggy jeans? The clothing would cause them to run at a much slower pace. They need to shed the clothing that restricts them so that they can run the race as effectively as they can. Can't you see that is how the average Christian is running the race for God today? They are so entangled by the things of this world, by the sins that they drag along with them, that they are not free to run. They try to run the race, but they are bogged down. Paul says in Ephesians 4:1, *"As a prisoner for the Lord, then, I urge you to live a life worthy of the calling you have received."* As Christians we have all received a calling to model a holy life and to serve and proclaim His Word. But instead, we get tangled in the things of this world. We worry so much about how we will be able to pay all of our bills, we worry if everything will come together for the party we are throwing, or if our favorite sports team will win the big game. How often do we contemplate the salvation of millions of souls each day going to hell? Our thoughts and concerns are on maintaining and gaining worldly wealth, and not on the race God has called us to run. When I realized that, it cut me like a knife. I'm letting this world and its cares distract me or entangle me from my true calling. I should be concerned a lot more about the salvation of souls, than I am about getting the next thing that I want. That is the sneaky thing about sin—

it easily entangles us. It comes without us knowing it. We don't necessarily invite sin into our lives—it sneaks in to bog us down and slow us up in our race for God. Free yourself from the world and from sins that easily entangle you, so that you can be an effective runner for the Lord.

My Testimony

I have a burden to share this message, because I remember the time when I realized I wasn't running the race God wanted me to run. I accepted Christ into my life when I was 14 years old. I grew up in a Christian home and I always knew that following God was the life I wanted to lead. But the problem was that I had a religion, not a relationship with Christ. After I was baptized, I still did not read God's Word or pray daily. My behaviors were relatively good in comparison with the culture that I lived in, but as I see now, in God's standard, I was still living according to my selfish desires.

In college, as I was walking to get my mail, an older gentleman who was working

> **But the problem was that I had a religion, not a relationship with Christ.**

for the Gideon's, handed me a little New Testament Bible. I grew up in a church home, so I had many Bibles. However, I didn't say anything because I didn't want to hurt his feelings. I took the Bible from him and shoved it in the side pocket of my backpack, thinking that there was no way I would ever read it.

Fast forward a couple of years to the summer after I graduated from college. I was asked to play on a small college all-star baseball team that would travel around Europe for 3 weeks. Of course I accepted! When

I was over there, I quickly realized that this wasn't a Christian baseball team. I was completely taken back by the lifestyle that most of these guys lived. While we were over there, I heard cursing all the time, drinking was legal and done frequently, and a few of the guys even did drugs and visited prostitutes. Seeing how these guys lived and the choices that they made, really drew me much closer to God. I went back into my room one night, and looked in my suitcase for my Bible. But as I told you earlier, I didn't read my Bible, so I didn't take my Bible with me to Europe. However, as I was looking in my book bag in the side pocket, there was the small Gideon's New Testament. I started to read it, and I have made it a priority from that time on to be in the Word of God every day.

That was the defining moment for me when I said, "OK God, I want to run your race. I will shed my sinful desires and start being obedient to you." I know that there are many people who are reading my testimony who have the same attitude today that I used to have regarding my relationship with God. They want to follow God, but it is not their first priority. We will follow God when it is convenient for us or when we have the time to do so. But God wants to be our first priority; He wants to be our first allegiance. I plead with you to join me and run the race that God has marked out for us. I never have regretted the day I started to run this race! And I am sure that you would not regret running this race either. Come on, I will help you get started.

chapter 2

Signing Up To Run The Race

There was a man one time who prayed, "Lord help me win the lottery." A woman overheard the man's prayer and asked him, "How many tickets did you buy?" To which the man replied, "I didn't purchase any."

Now, I am not advising you by any means to buy a lottery ticket, but how can the man expect to win the lottery if he didn't purchase any tickets? In the same way, how can we win a race if we never sign up to run the race? You have to actually be in the race if you want to receive the prize. Let's look at a man in Matthew 19 who chooses not to run the race that Jesus asks him to run.

> *16 Now a man came up to Jesus and asked, "Teacher, what good thing must I do to get eternal life?"*
> *17 "Why do you ask me about what is good?" Jesus replied. "There is only One who is good. If you want to enter life, obey the commandments."*
> *18 "Which ones?" the man inquired. Jesus replied, "'Do not murder, do not commit adultery, do not steal, do not give false testimony, 19 honor*

your father and mother,' and 'love your neighbor as yourself.'"

20 "All these I have kept," the young man said. "What do I still lack?"

21 Jesus answered, "If you want to be perfect, go, sell your possessions and give to the poor, and you will have treasure in heaven. Then come, follow me."

22 When the young man heard this, he went away sad, because he had great wealth.

Trying to win the race on our own

This passage starts out with a rich man coming to Jesus. He has a burning question on his mind. It should be a question every person on earth should want to know the answer to. *"How do I obtain eternal life?"* We all need to see that this earthly life is going to come to an end, so how can I make sure I have eternal life in heaven on the other side of the grave? Look closely at how this man phrases this question in verse 16. "What good thing must I do to get eternal life?" He misunderstands how to get eternal life. He says what <u>good thing</u> do I need to do? Eternal life is only by the grace of God, not by the good things that we do. A lot of people think in the same way that this rich man thinks. "I will earn my way to heaven. I will do good things." People often try to figure out the minimum they have to do and still make it to heaven. You can tell that this man is not willing to sacrifice very much. I can almost hear him say, "Just give me a list of the things that I need to do—Give $5000 to the poor, help 20 people, go to the temple services every week, do some volunteer work every month. Let me know the good things I need to do!" Jesus goes along with the man and says, "Keep the commandments." Jesus lists off part of the 10 commandments that deals with how to treat your fellow man and excludes the commandments about walking in a relationship with God. The rich man says, "I have followed these commandments." You would think he would feel pretty good right about now. "Yes! I have kept the commandments which Jesus just talked about. I'm going to make it to heaven." But he didn't walk away. He knew there was something more. Verse 20 says, *"'All these I have kept,' the young man said. 'What do I still lack?'"* He knew there was more than just being good. No one is going to make it to heaven by just being good, because none of us follow the 10 commandments perfectly. If I asked you today, "How well do you keep the 10 commandments?" how would you answer? Jesus says if you have lust in your heart—you've committed adultery.[3] He also says if you have hate in your heart—you are guilty of murder.[4] Have you ever stolen anything—a pencil or a quarter? Right there I have to admit that I am an adulterer, murder, and a thief at heart. Do you really want your entrance into heaven being based on whether or not you keep the 10 commandments? I don't. This just proves you can live a pretty clean life and not make it into heaven because you are trying to earn salvation by the good things you do, instead of being in a relationship with Jesus.

How many sins does it take for us to deserve hell?—ten, one hundred, one thousand, or one million sins until we deserve hell? No, all it takes is one sin and we deserve to spend eternity in hell. ONE SIN! When Adam and Eve were in the garden, they sinned one time and that one sin brought death. We sin once and we deserve the consequences of sin—spiritual death (separation from God). How many of us have sinned at least once? All of us have sinned. Romans 3:23 says, *"for all have sinned and fall short of the glory of God."* This is a verse we need to drill into our minds. We need to recognize that we have fallen short of God's standards.

Many people have the rich man's philosophy to eternal life—"I can earn it. If I do more good things than I do bad things, or if I go to church so many times or attend Sunday school or Bible studies, then I am alright." These things are good (we need to do them)—but they all fall short of getting us into heaven.

> A man woke up in the middle of the night and he smelled gas coming from the gas lines. He was too tired to try to fix it so he got some of his wife's perfume and sprayed half the bottle to cover the smell of the gas. The next morning there was someone from the county morgue there to haul their bodies out of the house.[5]

You may be able to cover the smell of gas by using perfume, but the consequences of gas, which is death, cannot be covered by perfume. In the same way, we too often try to cover up our sins to make it seem that they are not that bad. We try to cover our sins by doing good works. The sin is still there, but to us and to those around us it looks like it is not there. Our good works have covered it up pretty well, but the deadly consequence of our sin will come through. You cannot cover sin with good works. The only way to deal with sin is to come before Jesus and ask Him to take it away.

Sin, which is covered up and not dealt with, brings death! Romans 6:23, *"For the wages of sin is death, but the gift of God is eternal life in Christ Jesus our Lord."* Wages are something we earn. The wages of sin is death. We earn or deserve death. But a gift is something freely given to us. We get the free gift of eternal life because Jesus was willing to die in our place.

This rich man knew he still lacked something even though he kept all these commandments. He was still missing grace— he was missing a relationship with

> **How many sins does it take for us to deserve hell?—ten, one hundred, one thousand, or one million sins until we deserve hell? No, all it takes is one sin and we deserve to spend eternity in hell.**

Jesus Christ. Jesus tells us the one and only way to make it to heaven in John 14:6. *"Jesus answered, 'I am the way and the truth and the life. No one comes to the Father except through me.'"* Jesus makes it very clear—there is no good thing that you can do which will get your ticket punched to heaven. You must surrender your life to Christ and follow him. People talk about the sweet old lady who is nice to everybody and helps people out—am I trying to say that she is not going to heaven if she doesn't accept Jesus into her life? Yes, that is the case. The Bible says she has sin in her life and the only way to wash it away is to accept Jesus' work on the cross. God created us because He so desperately wanted to have a relationship with us. But when man sinned, that brought separation from God. He endured the cruel cross to restore that relationship with you again. It's not about your good deeds, it is about making him Lord of your life.

God made it very clear what He thought about sin in the very beginning. Back in the beginning, God told Adam and Eve, do not eat of the fruit in the middle of the garden. They could eat <u>any</u> of the fruit in the whole entire garden except from the tree of the Knowledge of Good and Evil.[6] But they disobeyed God and ate from it. God kicked them out of the garden. Some people may think God was too hard on Adam and Eve. "Isn't that an overreaction by God? All they did was eat a piece of fruit that they shouldn't have, and God kicked them out of the garden. Just a piece of fruit! What harm is there in disobeying God in that little act?" But God knew that sin and rebellion is progressive. They disobeyed God and ate a piece of fruit, and in <u>the next generation</u> we see Cain murdering his brother Abel. And look at the condition of the world now. Just because Adam and Eve ate one seemingly harmless fruit...this world is full of murders, sexual predators, sexual immorality, homosexuality, greed, stealing, lying, and ungodliness of all kinds. It came from one decision to eat a harmless piece of fruit.

Some Christians are living their lives like their sin is not that bad. "I don't have to die to this sin, what is wrong with me doing this one little thing? I know I am disobeying God, but this is a little sin that hardly affects anything." That is Satan whispering in your ear just like he did with Eve. I caution us all to think about approaching any sin as if it is not that bad. Sin progresses and before you know it, the devil has got you in a spot you never thought you would be in. Do you think Adam and Eve would have eaten the fruit if they knew one of their sons would kill the other? Do you think they would have eaten the fruit if they would have caught a glimpse of our world today? Sin looks pleasing to the eye at the time…but it leads you on a pathway to destruction. People have been deceived by the devil long enough thinking a piece of forbidden fruit will make them happy. The Bible shows the only way to have joy in your heart is to truly die with Christ and quit living for your selfish nature.

What a blessing God gave the human race by kicking

> *Some Christians are living their lives like their sin is not that bad. "I don't have to die to this sin, what is wrong with me doing this one little thing? I know I am disobeying God, but this is a little sin that hardly affects anything."*

Adam and Eve out of the garden. It may have been a form of punishment or discipline for disobedience, but we now see it is for our own good. What if God would have allowed Adam and Eve to stay in the garden? They might have eaten from the tree of Eternal Life. They would have lived forever. Could you imagine living in our aches and pains, bearing this sinful body forever? Praise the Lord that God cares enough for us to discipline us when we sin and to provide the sacrifice to wash away our sin.

We are all sinners and need Christ's cleansing work on the cross. Adam and Eve's sin has been passed down to each and every one of us. We were born in sin. Psalm 51:5 says, *"Surely I was sinful at birth, sinful from the time my mother conceived me."* We all need to see that we were born with a sinful nature. A rebellious nature handed down to us by our first parents, Adam and Eve.

The Bible clearly shows that sin is rebellion against

God. Colossians 1:21-22 says, *"Once you were alienated from God and were enemies in your minds because of your evil behavior. But now he has reconciled you by Christ's physical body through death to present you holy in his sight, without blemish and free from accusation."* Do you hear that strong language? We were enemies of God because we chose to follow our own sinful desires instead of living out the truth of God's Word. I can just imagine what God thinks when he looks around at the lives of church going people today. I think James 4:4 tells God's attitude towards "worldly" Christians. *"You adulterous people, don't you know that friendship with the world is hatred toward God? Anyone who chooses to be a friend of the world becomes an enemy of God."* There are many people who pretend to live a holy life on Sunday, but live like the devil the rest of the week. People come to church on Sunday, singing praises to God, but leave with a hard, unforgiving and rebellious heart—not willing to surrender their plans to the control of the Almighty God.

Today, if you haven't already, choose to live out what you say you believe. Surrender your whole life to him, and stop being an enemy to God by your lifestyle. Run the race the way God wants you to run. You cannot run a race unless you first sign up to be a part of it. Pray with me as we begin this race.

Lord Jesus,
I confess my sin. I have rebelled against you and have chosen my way over your way.
I thank you for dying upon the cross for my sin, and for giving me eternal life.
I know I am holy in your sight, not because of my good works, but by the precious blood of Christ.

Lord, today I want to start living for you. I give you total control of my life. Help me to look more like you each and every day.
In Jesus' name, Amen.

If you just prayed that prayer, congratulations! You are now in the most important race man can ever be in! Let's go train for the race.

chapter 3

Train For The Race

If we are committed to running the race, then we need to prepare for the race. Paul gives us some great advice in 1 Corinthians 9:24-27.

> *24 Do you not know that in a race all the runners run, but only one gets the prize? Run in such a way as to get the prize. 25 Everyone who competes in the games goes into strict training. They do it to get a crown that will not last; but we do it to get a crown that will last forever. 26 Therefore I do not run like a man running aimlessly; I do not fight like a man beating the air. 27 No, I beat my body and make it my slave so that after I have preached to others, I myself will not be disqualified for the prize.*

The people of Corinth could understand well this image about a race, because every other year they would hold the Isthmian games in their city—which are very similar to our Olympic games. They would compete in many different events to win a pine wreath. Obviously, this prize would fade away and not last very long. It is the same way with the prizes that we win in our events now. In our lives we win worldly prizes such as trophies, plaques, ribbons, and certificates. These prizes do not last either. They will break, rust, get scratched up, and tear…but in the race that we run as Christians, the prize will last for eternity. We get a crown that will last forever. So why do we chase after the prizes that don't last, instead of putting our energy toward getting one that will never wear out?

I don't think Paul is trying to say that only one person will win the Christian race and get the heavenly prize…but what he is saying is that not everyone who starts the race will get the prize. Some will be disqualified because they don't follow the rules, others may quit running the race and not finish. Don't take the race for granted. Run like you want the prize.

Train for the race

Verse 25 says, *"Everyone who competes in the games goes into strict training."* You don't see people decide the week before the Olympics that they want to compete in the games. They go into strict training. They dedicate their whole lives to the goal of competing in the games. While you and I may be sitting on the couch eating bon-bons and sipping sodas…they are working out at the gym, perfecting their skills and working on their weaknesses. If you want to win the race, you need to work at it. People work extremely hard in the gym just to win a little gold medal. As Christians, how hard do we work? How much time do we invest to train ourselves to run this Christian race effectively? To train for this race, we need to dig into the Word of God, pray, memorize scripture, go to church and Sunday school. We do whatever we can do to strengthen our spiritual muscles and perfect the skill of living for God.

One thing that is necessary for training is motivation. People are not going to put the time into training when they are not excited about the prize. People wouldn't train as hard as they do for the Olympics, if the prize was a lollipop. "If you train hard for 20 years you might win this cherry flavored lollipop." No. They train hard for the gold medal and to represent their country. We need to train hard because we get eternal life and we represent God. Think about this…how we train for the race, tells us a lot about how we feel about the race. If the race is important with an important prize we will work hard to get it. If we care little about the race and the prize—we will put little effort into it. How do you value the Christian race? How hard are you training for it?

In the small town that I live in, I see a guy out in his garden every time I drive by. He is an older gentleman that puts in at least 4 to 6 hours every day in his garden. He is pulling the weeds, putting on bug spray, and watering the plants. There are other people who I know

> *…how we train for the race tells us a lot about how we feel about the race. If the race is important with an important prize we will work hard to get it.*

that plant the garden in the spring and go out later in the summer to get the food. Other than those two times, they are not out in the garden. Who is going to have the better harvest? I think it is quite obvious. The more time you put in, the more you will get out of it. That is the same way with God's Word. If you don't take time to read it, how can you expect to bear spiritual fruit? We get sucked into our culture's idea of what a Christian is. Culture says a Christian is anybody who goes to church or anybody who says they believe in God. But we should not conform to their definition of a Christian. People don't read the Bible daily because they don't see a lot of other people doing it. Nobody memorizes Bible verses because they don't hear many other people doing it. No one forgives very easily because they don't witness many others doing it. Basically said, "No one grows in their walk with God, because they are not seeing anybody else growing in their walk with God." It doesn't matter if no one else in my church reads their Bible daily or memorizes scripture; I know I need to! We should not look to our culture to define what a Christian is. We should be students of God's Holy Word.

To train for this race we need to be in the Word of God every day. Why would I not want to read this wonderful book? The Bible is God's love letter to man. God tells man that He loves us so much that He is willing to come down and die upon a cross to save us. When my wife and I were dating, we lived three and a half hours away from each other. Every day we would email back and forth. Those were my daily electronical love notes with the one that I loved. How do you think I accepted those emails? "I don't want to read this. It looks pretty long. I will set this off to the side. Maybe I will get to this next week?" No way! I was reading that letter right away. I would study every sentence thinking about what she was trying to say when she used certain words to describe how she felt. I confess that I read those emails more than once. I would read them over and over again because they brought me joy to know that someone cared so much about me. In the same way, I have fallen in love with God's Word. God is someone that I truly love and I care about what He says about our relationship. Just to read about how much He loves me, gives me an incredible amount of hope to continue running the race through the daily trials that I face.

I have heard many people say that they can be a good Christian without going to church or reading the Bible regularly. Then they will ask me that question. "Can someone be an effective Christian without reading the Word of God or going to church?" A question I like to ask back to them is, "Can a doctor be an effective doctor without reading his medical books or attending seminars?" I don't think I would like to have that kind of doctor working on me. We need to train to run the race we are called to run.

Disciplined for the race

Athletes who compete are considered very disciplined people. There are times when they don't feel like working out that day. "I am tired today. I want to skip a day and watch movies instead." They may feel that way, but they are pushed on because they are motivated by the goal, to win a gold medal. In the race that we run, it is going to be the same way. There are going to be days that I am going to be thinking, "I don't want to read the Bible. I don't feel like praying today. It has been a long day—I just want to go to bed." I might say, "I don't feel like getting up and going to church today. I would rather hang out with my friends every night instead of taking time to really train for this Christian race I'm running."

A person competing in the Olympics probably trains 6 to 8 hours a day or more. And how much does the average Christian train for this important race he runs?—maybe 4 or 5 minutes a day? As Christians, we need to be spending many hours in God's Word and prayer throughout the week. It's not easy…that is why it is called discipline, because it makes you overcome your natural feelings to do something else. Over the course of my life I have lifted weights many times with the goal of keeping at it and getting stronger. I have never been disciplined enough to keep at it. I didn't feel like going to lift one day, so I didn't. The next day something came up and I didn't have time to lift. Before you know it, it had been several weeks since I lifted. So I stopped lifting. Could you imagine how much stronger I would be today if I would have continued to lift for the last 10 years? But I sacrificed that because I was not disciplined and wasn't motivated enough to see those results. And I have to live with what I have. In the same way, could you imagine where you can be a year from now if you were disciplined to read the Bible every day? Just think, in 5 years you would be a spiritual giant. You would have Bible knowledge you didn't think you could ever know and your faith would be much stronger. Or you could go on being undisciplined and not have those spiritual muscles. Discipline is doing the things you know you should do, even on the days you don't feel like it.

I played a lot of basketball growing up. There were many times I didn't feel like going to practices because I knew we would be running a lot. I was

A person competing in the Olympics probably trains 6 to 8 hours a day or more. And how much does the average Christian train for this important race he runs?

sore, I was tired, and to be truthful, I just didn't want to run. But I was part of a team and I was supposed to go. The team pushed me to put in the work to get ready for the big game. I believe we also can help each other grow in our walk with God. I have an accountability partner named Darrin. Every week we get together and quote memory verses to each other. I don't want him to find me unprepared saying, "Kurt how many verses did you memorize this week?" Hanging my head, "Umm, I didn't get any." Since I knew Darrin was going to ask me that question, I was motivated to get my verses memorized. We push each other. One week I had 4 verses, so Darrin came back the next week and memorized 6. I didn't want to be out done so I memorized 9. I was feeling pretty good about myself until he came back the next week with 16 verses. I conceded and told him he won! We memorized a lot of verses because we spurred each other on.

There was one year where Darrin and I did not meet. I think I memorized 8 verses the whole year. It is so much easier to slack off and not do something if you don't have someone there pushing you to do it. Find someone who will help you train to run this race. Make sure that person has a passion to run the race or they may slow you down.

I have heard people say, "I wish I knew the Bible as good as so and so over there. I wish I knew as many verses as they do." What they need to see is that that person over there put in a lot of time and hard work to be where he or she is at. What about you? Where do you want to be? You can achieve it if you are disciplined to seek God on a daily basis no matter how you are feeling or how busy your schedule is that day.

You need to know upfront that Satan does not want you to run this race. He will do all that he can to keep you from being disciplined with your relationship with God. He will be rejoicing when your life is so busy that you do not have time to spend with God. He will continually put thoughts in your head that you have too many other things to do than to sit quietly and wait upon the Lord. But the Bible gives us the opposite view. Isaiah 40:31, *"But they that wait*

> *We need to know upfront that Satan does not want you to run this race. He will do all that he can to keep you from being disciplined with your relationship with God.*

upon the LORD shall renew their strength; they shall mount up with wings as eagles; they shall run, and not be weary; and they shall walk, and not be faint."(KJV) It is spending time with the Lord that gives us the strength to run the race that is ahead of us that day.

Compete by the rules.

Verse 27 says, *"No, I beat my body and make it my slave so that after I have preached to others, I myself will not be disqualified for the prize."* Just because you run a race and you finish, doesn't mean that you will get the prize. Just ask the 2006 Tour de France winner— Floyd Landis. He won the bicycle race but they took the victory from him because he used illegal substances to help him perform better.

We can't live however we want to and still expect to get the prize. God has plans for the people who run this race. He has given us directions in His Word to help us run this race according to the rules. We also have His Spirit to guide us in the right paths we should take.

A good example of someone running his own race was King Saul in the Old Testament. He was the first King of Israel and he had the people's support and God's blessings. But that would soon change when he took matters in his own hands instead of waiting for God to act. In 1 Samuel 13 we see Saul's mistake.

> *5 The Philistines assembled to fight Israel, with three thousand chariots, six thousand charioteers, and soldiers as numerous as the sand on the seashore. They went up and camped at Micmash, east of Beth Aven. 6 When the men of Israel saw that their situation was critical and that their army was hard pressed, they hid in caves and thickets, among the rocks, and in pits and cisterns. 7 Some Hebrews even crossed the Jordan to the land of Gad and Gilead.*
>
> *Saul remained at Gilgal, and all the troops with him were quaking with fear. 8 He waited seven days, the time set by Samuel; but Samuel did not come to Gilgal, and Saul's men began to scatter. 9 So he said, "Bring me the burnt offering and the fellowship offerings." And Saul offered up the burnt offering. 10 Just as he finished making the offering, Samuel arrived, and Saul went out to greet him.*
>
> *11 "What have you done?" asked Samuel.*
>
> *Saul replied, "When I saw that the men were scattering, and that you did not come at the set time, and that the Philistines were assembling at Micmash, 12 I thought, 'Now the*

*Philistines will come down against
me at Gilgal, and I have not sought
the LORD's favor.' So I felt compelled
to offer the burnt offering."*

*[13] "You acted foolishly," Samuel
said. "You have not kept the command
the LORD your God gave you; if
you had, he would have established
your kingdom over Israel for all
time. [14] But now your kingdom will
not endure; the LORD has sought
out a man after his own heart and
appointed him leader of his people,
because you have not kept the
LORD's command."*

Saul was supposed to wait for Samuel and
Samuel was going to lead the burnt offering. However,
Saul found himself in leadership now and he thought
that he was the head of Israel. He saw his men start to
get worried and scatter, so he took matters into his own
hands. He disobeyed, thinking that as the leader of Israel
he could do that. If only Saul would have stopped and
remembered that it was God who lifted him up to be King
of Israel, and it was God who was in charge. God would
be the One who would take care of his people. But in our
humanness we can see why Saul did what he did. He was
looking at some impossible odds with an army coming at
him, so he thought he had to do something. It can be the
same way in our lives. We get backed into a corner and
instead of waiting patiently and being obedient to God;
we try to work the situation out with our own intellect.
This passage shows us the result of Saul's disobedience

to God. His kingdom was going to be taken away from him. If he would have followed the Lord, the kingdom would have remained in his family.

There was another time that Saul did not follow God's Word completely. In 1 Samuel 15:3, Samuel tells Saul God's plans for the fight ahead, "Now go, attack the Amalekites and totally destroy

Obedience is what God really wants from us. He doesn't want you to lie and cheat and steal so you can bring a bigger tithe to church to give to Him. He doesn't want you to read His Word for hours on end and then forget to look after the poor and hurting in the world.

everything that belongs to them. Do not spare them; put to death men and women, children and infants, cattle and sheep, camels and donkeys." The word of God was plain to Saul. Go attack the Amalekites and totally destroy everything. But in 1 Samuel 15, Samuel approaches Saul after the battle.

> [13] When Samuel reached him, Saul said, "The LORD bless you! I have carried out the LORD's instructions."
> [14] But Samuel said, "What then is this bleating of sheep in my ears? What is this lowing of cattle that I hear?"
> [15] Saul answered, "The soldiers brought them from the Amalekites; they spared the best of the sheep and cattle to sacrifice to the LORD your

*God, but we totally destroyed the
rest."*

[16] *"Stop!" Samuel said to Saul.
"Let me tell you what the LORD said
to me last night."*

"Tell me," Saul replied.

God was angry with Saul because Saul didn't follow His instructions. Saul was confused because he thought he did what God asked him to do. He went to war and defeated the Amalekites, but God's instructions were clear. He told Saul to totally destroy everything, but Saul reasoned with himself that it wouldn't hurt for him to keep the best things of the land. "I can even sacrifice some of these nice things to the Lord. Won't He be happy with these grand sacrifices that we are bringing?" But what God wanted more than any type of sacrifice, was for Saul to be obedient.

Obedience is what God really wants from us. He doesn't want you to lie and cheat and steal so you can bring a bigger tithe to church to give to Him. He doesn't want you to read His Word for hours on end and then forget to look after the poor and hurting in the world. We shouldn't preach the Word of God to others, but then fall short ourselves because we do not live out what we preach. What He wants from us is obedience!

He calls us to this race, and He has the rules that He wants us to follow. Do not disqualify yourself from getting this great prize.

chapter 4

Perserverance

There once was a man who won state in running the 100-meter dash. Now he was running the first leg of a relay race, in which every runner was required to run 400 meters. He was boasting that no one was going to be able to beat him since he was a state champion. The starter fired his gun, and the man was way ahead after 100 meters, but after 200 meters he slowed down, and after 300 meters he was holding his side and barely jogging. All the runners passed him up and he was the last one to pass off his baton. It was a good lesson for everyone who was there. It makes little difference if you hold the record for the 100-meter dash if the race is 400-meters long.[7]

Perseverance is part of this Christian race we are talking about. An important thing we need to see is that the Christian race is a marathon and not a sprint. The Christian race is not a race you run for 2 or 3 years. It is not even a race you run for 20 or 25 years. It is a race that you run for a lifetime. This race that you are running is not an easy race. Many become faint hearted before they reach the finish line. I think of Judas Iscariot. He ran the race. He sought out Jesus to become one of his disciples. He went out with the other disciples and healed the sick and preached about Jesus, but he got sidetracked on his race. He began to steal money out of the disciples' treasury.[8] He betrayed Jesus for money.[9]

Judas let the world entangle him and he didn't keep his focus upon Jesus.

The key to any race is to finish. We need to persevere when the going gets tough. The author of Hebrews gives us a little insight about how to reach the finish line. Let me share Hebrews 12 with you again.

> [1] *Therefore, since we are surrounded by such a great cloud of witnesses, let us throw off everything that hinders and the sin that so easily entangles, and let us run with perseverance the race marked out for us.* [2] *Let us fix our eyes on Jesus, the author and perfecter of our faith, who for the joy set before him endured the cross, scorning its shame, and sat down at the right hand of the throne of God.* [3] *Consider him who endured such opposition from sinful men, so that you will not grow weary and lose heart.*

Pain in the race

When we run this race for the Lord, we need to know that it is not always going to be easy. The race is marked out for us, but we will still have to persevere through difficult times. When you are in a race, sometimes you get some aches and pains, but you don't stop running the race. You keep going, despite the pain you feel. If you don't finish, you don't receive the prize. In a race, you have hills that you go over. Going down the hill is easy, but going up the hill is very tough. Again, life is just like that. Sometimes life will be easier and things will just fall into place. There will be other times when it is going to take every ounce that we have to make it through the day. We all have hard times in our lives; that is why the Bible repeatedly tells us to persevere. The question is, how do we deal with the hard times that come into our lives?

People have done amazing things in this life because they persevere and do not lose heart. They don't let difficulties distract them from their goals. The author of Hebrews says in verse 1, "*and let us run with perseverance the race marked out for us.*" Don't give up! It is easy to enter a race and get at the starting line and take off at a dead sprint when the shot is fired. But it is when we are in the middle of the race that it starts to get tougher. You might get a side ache, your legs might hurt…you are wondering, "Why in the world did I sign up for this race?" The Christian race can be the same way. When you first come to Christ, you may think, "I am on fire—I am running as fast as I can. This isn't so bad." Then the pain comes, and the struggles of life start to make you think, "Why is this race so important? I can quit this race right now if I want to. Maybe I should just slow my pace down and walk." We should not fool ourselves; this Christian race is going to be tough. You need to commit to finishing the race before you even start it. Because if you don't commit to the importance of finishing the race, when certain problems come your way, you will have thoughts of quitting. But if you say at the beginning, "I am not going to quit regardless of what happens," when those tough times actually come, you can lean back on what you said. You said you wouldn't quit. Too many people are quitting the most important race they will ever run. They turn from the Lord because life is hard and find themselves asking God, "How could you let life be this hard for me?"

I went to a Promise Keepers event with a couple guys from our church one year, and there was a speaker there named Dave Roever. He was a Vietnam Veteran who had a grenade blow up in his face

> *You need to commit to finishing the race before you even start it. Because if you don't commit to the importance of finishing the race, when certain problems come your way, you will have thoughts of quitting.*

and his face was completely disfigured, but he didn't let that keep him down. He easily could have let that episode ruin his life, but now he is a nationally known speaker and he brings many people to the Lord. He encourages people to live the hand that they have been dealt in life. He didn't want to be disfigured, but he wasn't going to complain about it. He was going to make the best of it. What is your outlook when you go through bad times? Are you discouraged, wanting to give up? Tough times can either crush our spirits, or they can make us stronger.

Fix your eyes on Jesus

When we go through difficulties, we need someone to help us through. Verse 2 tells us where our focus should be. *"Let us fix our eyes on Jesus, the author and perfecter of our faith, who for the joy set before him endured the cross, scorning its shame, and sat down at the right hand of the throne of God."* Jesus can help us through our difficult times. Jesus provides us with a great example of perseverance through difficulties. Obviously, Jesus faced many difficulties in life; none of them were bigger than the one being led to the cross. The middle of verse 2 says this about Jesus, *"…who for the joy set before him endured the cross."* Jesus saw the final outcome. He could look past the cross and see the salvation of people who believed in him. Jesus was able to see past the mocking, the beating, the crown of thorns, and the hours nailed to the cross. He saw that the cross was His immediate future, but he realized that it was not the end of the story. He realized that what lay beyond the cross was eternal life for millions of precious souls who would surrender their lives to him. Jesus saw the joy that lay beyond the cross, and it made the cross worth bearing.

We need to look beyond our troubling circumstances to the joy that lies beyond. It is then that we will be able to endure the hardships in Christ because we see the results of staying in the race. Satan's greatest trick is to get your focus off of Jesus and have you focus on your problems. Don't take your eyes off of Jesus or you will be like Peter when he was walking on the water toward Jesus.[10] Peter took his eyes of off Jesus and he sunk, but when his focus was on Jesus he walked on the water. Jesus is our focus. Keep your eyes on the goal, the finish line, and not on the pain of the moment.

If you are following the Lord with your life, Satan is going to try to trip you up. If he can wound

> *Jesus is our focus. Keep your eyes on the goal, the finish line, and not on the pain of the moment.*

you or talk you into quitting, he will win a victory for his kingdom. But we need to shake off the hurts and pains and keep running this race with perseverance.

There was a story of a dog that lived on a farm.

He would run and play all day—but one day he fell down into an open well. He was down about 15 feet—the farmer tried and tried to get his dog out…but he couldn't. The opening of the hole was too small. The farmer had no choice but to bury the dog and fill the hole with dirt. The farmer started shoveling dirt into the hole. The dog was squealing because the dirt fell from 15 feet in the air and it really hurt. But you know what happened? The dog shook off the dirt and stood on top of it. The dog continued to shake off the dirt that came down on him and stepped up on it. After a while, the dog was up high enough to jump out of the hole. The dirt that came to bury him, eventually helped him.[11]

There have been times in my life where I have asked myself the question, "How committed am I to running the race God has for me?" I felt God's call to be a pastor many years ago now, but let me tell you that this was not the race I would have chosen to run. I was at a fork in the road as I was asking myself, "Will I choose God's race or run my own race?" My race seemed to be a lot easier and more in my comfort zone, but my race took my eyes off of Jesus and put them on myself. So I chose God's race. There have been many challenging times in running this race, but God has always supplied the grace needed to help me through. Sometimes we have to change our plans and our dreams to run the race God has called us to run.

Examples of those who went before us
When we run this race of faith, we have examples to lead us. Verse 1 says, *"…we are surrounded by such a great cloud of witnesses".* Who are those witnesses? The cloud of witnesses mentioned here are the people listed in the previous chapter. Hebrews 11 is considered

the Hall of Fame of faith. These are men who trusted God and took Him at His Word even when there was no evidence to back it up. Noah did not build the ark when he saw the rain clouds coming. God called him to build it before people even knew what rain was. Up to this point, there had never been rain falling from the sky. Yet with the birds chirping and the sun shining, Noah obeyed the Lord and built an ark. There are many other stories in Hebrews 11 that display complete trust in God. We are not always going to see why God is asking us to do certain things or why He is leading our lives in a certain direction. There are some things we may never understand on this side of heaven. Hebrews 11:13 says, *"All these people were still living by faith when they died. They did not receive the things promised; they only saw them and welcomed them from a distance. And they admitted that they were aliens and strangers on earth."* Noah, Abraham, Joseph, Moses, and many others only saw the promise in the distance while on the earth. The earth was not their home. The promise was in the unseen. We also need to see that we are strangers on this earth and we need

> *We are not always going to see why God is asking us to do certain things or why He is leading our lives in a certain direction. There are some things we may never understand on this side of heaven.*

to persevere until we are at home with our God. Then we will understand all the trials we went through on this earth.

These examples of faith really encourage me. I want to live my life in full abandonment to God like they did. But I think some people are discouraged by this Hebrews 11 passage. They can't see how they could be anything like the people in this list. We need to see that these people are ordinary people that God made extraordinary. Without God's Spirit working in them, they would be like your average church attendee. Sitting on the pew thinking, "God is a safe God." These people knew that God was an All-Powerful God and that He would do amazing things through them. Do not be discouraged by these great men of faith. Look at the people on this list. Moses was a murderer, Noah was a drunkard, David was an adulterer and murderer, and Abraham was a liar. These people are not heroes of the faith because they are perfect, but because they worked with God in His perfect work. God has shown us examples of how He can take ordinary people who trust in Him and bring Him glory. God can also use you mightily for His kingdom work.

Tap into God's strength

There is no way that we can run the race that God has for us in our own strength. If we are left by ourselves, we will be entangled by sin and frustrated with our lack of strength to live a pleasing life to God. Fortunately for us, God has given us the power to run His race, if we only accept it.

> During the depression, a man named Yates owned a ranch. Mr. Yates wasn't able to make enough on his ranching operation to make his payments to the bank for the land, so he was in danger of losing his ranch. With little money for clothes or food,

his family had to live on government subsidy. Day after day, as he grazed his sheep over those rolling Texas hills, there was no doubt that he was greatly troubled about how he would pay his bills. 5, 10, 15 years went by and he was still struggling to get by. Then people from the oil company came and took readings. They asked permission to drill a well in his land, and he agreed. They drilled into his ground and hit oil. They got 80,000 barrels of oil a day. They dug many more wells that produced twice as much as the first one. 30 years later they were still getting oil. Mr. Yates owned it all. What we need to see is, the day Mr. Yates purchased the land he had received the oil and mineral rights. A multimillionaire…yet he was living for so long in poverty.[12]

Why did Mr. Yates choose to live in poverty when he was so rich? Because he didn't know the oil was there. Even though he owned it, he could not see it. This man had the land and he was using it…but not to its full potential. There was so much more there that he could have. It is the same with us. Many Christians are living in spiritual poverty. They are entitled to the gifts of the Holy Spirit and his energizing power, but they are blinded to what the spirit can do. We know we have Jesus…but too many of us don't see the hidden gift of the Spirit.

As we start section two of this book, remember

that there is so much richness in the Christian life that we haven't tapped into yet. Let us be a hero of faith to those who come behind us!

PART 2

Running The Race

So then, just as you received Christ Jesus as Lord, continue to live in him, rooted and built up in him, strengthened in the faith as you were taught, and overflowing with thankfulness.

— Colossians 2:6-7

chapter 5

Starting The Race

It is interesting that I am currently writing this book about running the race. Within weeks of this book's release I will be running my first marathon. It is not really an organized marathon—it will just be with my best friend, Michael, and we will be running along the back roads of Illinois. I have always talked about running a marathon some day, but up to this point I never got around to it. So finally, I had to set a date to actually run the race, because I knew that "someday" may never come.

As I am writing this chapter, I am doing a lot of running to get ready for that big day. I ran/walked ten miles today and right now I am feeling every step of those ten miles! I can tell you with confidence that getting started is the hardest thing to do. It would be so easy to quit right now and say, "The marathon was a good idea, but it is not meant to be." No matter what you do, getting started is the hardest part. If you lift weights, the next day your muscles are going to be yelling at you for using them too much. You will be tempted to stop lifting, but you need to keep going. The hard part is starting. Last week, I ran/walked ten miles, so I was hoping that today it would be a lot easier. But do you know what? One week didn't make the run much easier at all. The run was still hard and it also took determination on my part to finish the ten miles that I set out to run. I am sure it will take a lot more than two training sessions before it starts to get easier. When I made my first two-mile loop around the neighborhood, I wanted to quit a hundred times. That first lap was the hardest lap of the entire run. My body was not warmed up and was fighting me to give up and go in and watch TV and grab some snacks. Luckily, after the first lap, I finally started to hit my stride. I definitely want you to understand that getting started is the hardest part, because you have to discipline your body to do something that it doesn't want to do.

The same is true in our spiritual lives. The beginning of the race is going to be one of the most trying times because you are disciplining yourself to do something that you naturally wouldn't do on your own. You may come to Christ with great excitement and think that there is nothing too difficult about this new life in Christ. I challenge you to take another look at your life. Did it change at all from how you were living before you came to Christ? Most people think there is nothing hard about the Christian life because the only thing that changed was the label that they now wear. They are still the same people that they were before, but now they spend an hour at church. As you will see, there is far more to the Christian life than sitting through an hour long church service.

The beginning is the toughest part of God's race because it causes changes in the lives of faithful followers of Jesus. In

Most people think there is nothing hard about the Christian life because the only thing that changed was the label they now wear.

the second part of this book, you will read about many disciplines that need to change in a believer's life. How we handle our money, choosing to forgive and release bitterness, living sexually pure lives, and watching the words that we choose to use are all forms of discipline that we will need to continually work on. We willingly need to kill our flesh and our old ways, to start living the way that God wants us to live. Jesus says in Luke 9:23, *"...If anyone would come after me, he must deny himself and take up his cross daily and follow me."* Jesus says that we, being His followers, have to deny ourselves. It is a tough transition when we begin to lay down the desires that we have had since birth and start living in a totally new way that goes against our sinful nature. Don't think the beginning of the Christian walk will be easy, unless of course you choose to merge your old life together with the new life. If your behaviors don't change, then I guess it won't be that hard of a transition. But the problem is, you won't really be living for Christ! You would be living for yourself and following Christ when it is convenient for you.

It is going to take some work to grow in Christ, but the great thing is that it will be enjoyable work. You will enjoy the process of knowing God more and more. It is like the time I met my future wife. I didn't know her at all. I didn't completely know her after our first date. I didn't look around and say, "I wish I was like that older couple over there. I wish I knew this girl like they know each other." No, I treasured every moment getting to know her better each and every day. I looked forward to every phone call as well as every day that we could be together. I looked forward to doing nothing but being in her presence. That is the same joy we get in starting our relationship with God. We don't know Him as well as someone who has been following Him for 40 years, but there is the joy of learning new things about Him daily.

It doesn't matter that I don't know God as good as so and so; today is the special and memorable day I get to know more of Him.

The problem is that when people have been in a relationship for a long time, they tend to take that relationship for granted. Most marriages are not very strong today, because they lose the joy of dating. After marriage, they are done trying to learn more about their spouse. They get caught up in the everyday things of life, and they take their marriage for granted. Each day we can learn more and more about our spouse and we will never know them completely as long as we live. There are too many marriages in which people are dwelling with their spouse, but have let the love slip away. They don't take the precious time that is required to continue to build the relationship with them. In the same way, sometimes Christians take their relationship with Christ for granted. They were at one time on fire for God, but now they get caught up in the other things of life. They don't continue to grow in him daily. We could study the Bible every day and never come close to fully understanding who God truly is. Each and every one of us can know more about God today than we did yesterday. But we must have a desire to want to know Him.

We have someone in our congregation who just came to Christ several months ago. He is soaking in the Word of God and wanting to know more and more about it. He did not grow up learning the Bible stories and learning the ways that God wanted him to live. He commented to me one day, "I can't wait until I can get up and do something in front of the church like so and so is doing." He seemed down because he felt like he was way behind everyone else in knowing the things of God. Obviously it is great to know the Bible at an early age, but we must start where we find ourselves today. I encouraged him and said, "If you dig into the Bible daily, come to church, and attend a Bible study group; in a year you will probably have more knowledge than 75% of the people in the church." Unfortunately that is a sad fact. The church of God has become married to Christ, but they do not have the desire to see their relationship continue to grow in Him.

The church of God has become married to Christ, but they do not have the desire to see their relationship continue to grow in Him.

I read a story one time of a blind woman who really enjoyed her time with God. The only way she could read the Bible was with a Braille Bible. She would spend hours each day in God's Word. The problem became that her fingers were becoming calloused and the Braille was not as clear as it once was because of the many times her fingers ran over it. She got to the point where she didn't think she was going to be able to read the Word of God anymore. She brought the Bible up to her lips to kiss it goodbye, and she noticed that her lips were sensitive enough to make out the Braille letters. So she ended up reading the Word of God by rubbing her lips across the pages.

WOW! I absolutely love that story. Do we love the Word of God like that? We need to have a hunger to know God like this woman did. Too often Christians don't even take the time to read God's life changing Word. The Psalmist shows his desire for God's Word. Psalm 119:103 says, *"How sweet are your words to my taste, sweeter than honey to my mouth!"* He couldn't get enough of the Word of God. Let me ask you, "How often do you read the Word of God? Is it part of your everyday life?" There should be nothing more important happening in our lives that should take us away from that.

In life we get to choose the things that take up our time. We are so busy living our lives, that there is no time left to read the Bible. It is easy to say, "I will read the Bible when I have time." But as we all know, our lives are very full and we never have the time. We, as believers in Jesus Christ, need to make time to get directions for our lives. Titus 3:14 says, *"Our people must learn to devote themselves to doing what is good, in order that they may provide for daily necessities and not live unproductive lives."* If you were to measure your everyday life in the light of eternity, would you find that you are living a productive life? It is so easy to get caught up in the demands of the world, but remember the world is going to perish. Spend time doing things that will never perish. One of Satan's biggest tricks is to keep the people of God so busy that they don't have time to seek direction from God for their lives. How can we be God followers, if we don't even know where He wants to lead us?

> *"How often do you read the Word of God? Is it part of your everyday life?"*

As you read on in this book, please consider becoming more than a "Christian" in label only, and truly choosing to have a relationship with Him. Let your life be changed, so that you will be willing to deny yourself to please Him. You may be just starting this race, or perhaps you accepted Jesus Christ many years ago, but as you read you realize that you are not running the race that God has called you to—today is the day to begin a sold out life for your Savior. We need to live wholeheartedly for God today, because if we put it off any longer, "someday" may never come. A warning: Many people think they are running the race, yet they haven't even gotten up from the couch! Come on, let's get up and run the race God has called us too.

chapter 6

Being A Disciple

Jesus was not the first person to have disciples. Having disciples was a common practice in Bible days. We are told in the Bible that the Pharisees had disciples.[13] John the Baptist also had disciples.[14] Leaders attracted people who were serious about their teaching and outlook and they would train or mentor them. The word for disciple simply means learner. You as a disciple are learning from your leader. "Now in learning anything there is something to be understood, something to be grasped mentally. But we need to know that being a disciple is not just head knowledge only."[15]

Rabbi/Disciple Relationship

I want to spend a little bit of time giving you the background on a rabbi-disciple relationship. For those who are unfamiliar with the term rabbi, a rabbi is a teacher. Here is a little description of what a rabbi is looking for in a potential student.

In Bible days, kids would study the scriptures day after day. They would memorize the first 5 books of the Old Testament. Then, they would seek out a well known Rabbi and apply to become one of his disciples. By saying, "I want to become one of your disciples" that meant more than just learning what the Rabbi could teach him. The goal of a disciple was to be like the Rabbi, and to impact the world in the same way the Rabbi did. The Rabbi would only want to train a young man who could become like him. He would not waste time training the good intentioned student who did not have what it would take. So he would closely interrogate the young man on all the things he should have already learned. If he decided that the student was not the best student for these high standards, he would send him home with the words, "You obviously love God and know the Law but you do not have what it takes to be my disciple. Go home and learn the family business." And that was the end of that young man's ambitions. They would go home and be farmers, fishermen or whatever their family business was. But if the Rabbi believed that the student had what was needed, he would say to him, "Come, follow me." And the student would. He would probably have to leave his parents, his synagogue, his village, and travel around with that rabbi, learning how to do what the rabbi did. He would give up his whole life just to be like his rabbi. Young Jewish boys would dream of one day being offered such a position, but sadly, most arrived at age 15 knowing that they would never make it. They were just not good enough to be a disciple of any rabbi. It was an extreme privilege to have a rabbi teach you.[16]

Understanding this relationship, let's look at Jesus when He goes to the seashore to call Peter, Andrew, James and John to be his disciples. Matthew 4:19 says, "'Come, follow me,' Jesus said, 'and I will make you fishers of

> **The goal of a disciple was to be like the Rabbi, and to impact the world in the same way the Rabbi did.**

men.'" Jesus is calling Peter, Andrew, James & John to leave everything and follow Him. He's telling them, "I will be your rabbi, your teacher, and you will learn from me. Let down your nets and come and follow me." It says in the next verse, verse 20, *"At once they left their nets and followed him."* Think about the decision they were making. They would be leaving everything behind; their secure job, their homes, their family and friends. This passage says James and John just left their father on the boat as they went to follow Jesus. Jewish people believed strongly in respecting your elders, and honoring your father and mother. But when Jesus called them, they left their father. Their decision to follow Jesus was more important than any earthly relationship. In Luke 14:26 Jesus says, *"If anyone comes to me and does not hate his father and mother, his wife and children, his brothers and sisters—yes, even his own life—he cannot be my disciple."* Does Jesus really want us to hate our family? No, Jesus is exaggerating to show that He is the most important relationship you should have. You are to follow and please God before you please your spouse. God dictates your schedule, not your kids. God is the number one priority. This week I thought about how the disciples just dropped everything and followed Jesus. If Jesus came into my office and said, "Drop your pencil and paper and follow me." That would make it personal for me. Could I forsake all things and go? Could I get out of my office chair and leave my wife, my house, my possessions, my friends & family and go; not knowing when I would be coming back? This would be a great sacrifice. The disciples sacrificed greatly, but they counted it a high privilege that someone would actually want them to be a disciple. Jesus was not just anybody, but the one that John the Baptist said, "He is the Lamb of God, who takes away the sins of the world."[17] They have the best rabbi and teacher in the world.

So for the next 3 years, they followed Jesus day and night. Jesus taught them many things and they saw the power of God at work. But like all other rabbis, Jesus did not want to pass on knowledge only to his disciples; He also wanted them to act on that knowledge. He wanted them to take on His character. Jesus wanted them to be like Him. In Luke 6:40, Jesus says, *"A student is not above his teacher, but everyone who is fully trained will be like his teacher."* Take a close look at what that verse says. If you are fully trained by your teacher, you will be like him. You won't just know his teachings, but you will be like him. Certainly we need to be taught by God's Word so we can know more and more of the truth. But as a disciple of Jesus it is so much more than head knowledge. It is about taking on who He is, and having His character. We need to be more like Christ, being like the One we follow. This is an important point because back in Bible days, head knowledge was not enough. Rabbis did not want to pass on head knowledge—but a way of life. If you didn't live what they taught—you were not one of their disciples.

Once there was someone who was talking to a great scholar about a younger man. He said, "So and so tells me that he was one of your students."[18]

> **If you are fully trained by your teacher, you will be like him. You won't just know his teachings, but you will be like him.**

The scholar answered, "He may have attended my lectures, but he was not one of my students." The scholar didn't want to be associated with this man. This man heard the teachings of the scholar, but did not practice what the scholar taught. As I look at the American church, I can hear Jesus saying something similar. "They may attend church and hear from my word, but they are not my disciples." Jesus does tell us in Matthew 7:21, *"Not everyone who says to me, 'Lord, Lord,' will enter the kingdom of heaven, but only he who does the will of my Father who is in heaven."* The key phrase in this verse is, *"only he who does the will of my Father."* It is not just hearing the Word, but it is putting it into practice. We need to know the teachings of God, but then we also need to live them out! We need to be like Jesus.

God can transform anyone to be his disciple.

God proved He can transform anyone by the people He called to be his first disciples. They were not the cream of the crop. While all the other rabbis choose students who excelled in Bible knowledge, Jesus chose the ones you would least expect. Jesus could have chosen the smartest, richest, most well-connected people to join him in his ministry. But instead, he called the simple fishermen.[19] What this means for us is that God can use anyone. This passage is for all of us who think we are not good enough, smart enough, or rich enough to be used by Jesus. We are called into God's service, and God can use all of us. It does not matter where we come from, what the color of our skin is, what we do for a living, or what our GPA was in college. You may not know your Bible inside and out, but it all starts with a desire to follow Him and be used by him. If you truly become a disciple, and make Him number one in your life, I guarantee you will get to know Him better. You will not be able to put His Holy Word down.

We see in Matthew 4 that Jesus called 4 fishermen to be his disciples, but let's examine a couple of the other disciples. Within the smaller group of the twelve disciples of Jesus, we find Simon the zealot and Matthew the tax-collector—a Zealot and a tax collector? "Zealots and tax-collectors were at opposite ends of the spectrum. The zealots hated the Romans and did not want Rome to occupy the land of Israel. The zealots used terrorism and sabotage to try to get rid of the Romans."[20] Probably very similar to what the U.S. troops are faced with in Iraq and Afghanistan. The zealots hated the Roman Occupiers. "But on the other hand, the tax-collectors made lots of money working as tax collectors for Rome. They profited greatly from Rome's occupation. Yet Jesus called both the friend of Rome and the foe of Rome to be his disciples."[21] He is going to have them live together. I imagine even his disciples needed to hear Jesus words in John 13:35. Jesus says, *"By this all men will know that you are my disciples, if you love one another."*

As disciples, we need to love people even when we don't agree with them. It is interesting to see how many divisions there are with people who claim to follow Christ. At Boynton Mennonite Church, the church I preach at, we had an issue a few years back that divided a lot of people. We were part of the Olympia school district, and Olympia was going to close our local grade school and bus our kids to another grade school in the district. Some people thought we needed to connect with another district close by so that we could keep a local grade school in Hopedale, and others wanted to stay with the Olympia school district. We even had some people who were so worked up over this issue, that they left the church because they didn't like the fact that some people had different thoughts than they had. They couldn't associate with someone who thought differently. Other people divide themselves as Republican and Democrats. People are going to think differently than you think. I don't see anywhere in scripture where it says we all have to be Democrats, or we all have to want Olympia as our high school. But Jesus shows us that as disciples we can live with people we don't agree with.

But how do we know who Jesus' disciples are? In John 8:31-32, Jesus says, *"To the Jews*

A true disciple will sacrifice pleasures and desires to look like his teacher.

who believed him, Jesus said, 'If you hold to my teaching, you are really my disciples. Then you will know the truth, and the truth will set you free.'" If you hold to my teaching you are really my disciples. It doesn't come down to how much you know the scriptures, but it comes down to whether you are obedient to the Holy Scriptures. Is your life displaying Christ's likeness? When people look at your life, can they tell Jesus is your Rabbi, your Teacher? Do they see He is the Lord that you follow? A true disciple will sacrifice pleasures and desires to look like his teacher.

Draw New Maps

The Disciples left the familiar to go to the unknown. As fishermen, they always knew what tomorrow would bring. They were on their boat and doing what they knew. But if they left to follow Jesus, what would the next day bring? Who knows?

A seminary professor tells a story about Alexander the Great, that talented conqueror who conquered almost the entire known world by around the age of 30. One night he walked into the campfire where his well-trained generals often sat and celebrated their victories, expecting to hear again their confidence. But what he heard on this particular night was a good bit of anxiety and hesitation, and it concerned him, because they were to enter battle again the next day. He asked his general what was the matter. The general replied, "Sir, you asked us to break camp in the morning, and strike out into our next conquest."

"Yes?" said Alexander. "And isn't that what we've always done, time after time?"

"Yes, sir," replied the faithful

soldier, "but up until now, sir, we've followed our maps. Sir . . . tomorrow . . . we have no maps. We've conquered all we know; we don't know where we are going."

Alexander waited for a moment, and then announced, "Gentlemen! Tonight we sleep. In the morning, we break camp, and we walk into new territory . . . and conquer! Then, when we've done so . . . we'll draw the maps!"[22]

We will draw new maps. This is exactly what Jesus asked the fishing brothers to do, "Follow me into the unknown." And as a result of their faithfulness, they helped draw new maps for us, by writing what we know as the gospels and the New Testament. Let us take that next step of discipleship and leave a map for the next generation. There is a Christian song that the Gaither Vocal Band sings called, "Let all who come behind us find us faithful". Let the next generation be immersed in the gospel because we were faithful like the disciples and were will to abandon everything to follow Jesus. We need to set an example and leave a strong church for them—a map that points them to faith in Jesus Christ.

chapter 7

Covenant Relationship

In Ephesians 4:1 Paul says, *"As a prisoner for the Lord, then, I urge you to live a life worthy of the calling you have received."* We all have received a calling from God to live for him. When He becomes Lord of our lives, He expects us to live a certain way, just as God expected the Israelites to live a certain way in the Old Testament.

Old Covenant

Let's take a closer look at the covenant stipulations that God made with the people of Israel in the Old Testament. Deuteronomy 4:13, "He declared to you his covenant, the Ten Commandments, which he commanded you to follow and then wrote them on two stone tablets." Israel's part of the covenant was to keep the 10 commandments, but that was not all. Moses teaches them more of what God says throughout the book of Deuteronomy...and in Deuteronomy 29:1 it says, *"These are the terms of the covenant the Lord commanded Moses to make with the Israelites in Moab, <u>in addition</u> to the covenant he had made with them at Horeb."* So Moses taught them much more about God than just the 10 commandments—such as dietary laws (what they could eat and not eat), sacrificial laws (animal sacrifices they had to perform to please God), and civil laws. This was Israel's part of the covenant; this is what they had to follow. God's part of the covenant (what He agreed to) was to lead them into the Promise Land which flowed with milk and honey. God was going to provide them with a land that was filled with the best of everything. If Israel kept its part of the covenant, God was going to provide them with protection and blessings. He promises to watch over them. Israel was excited about living in the great Promise Land with the best of everything and knowing that God was watching over them. Their response to the covenant God was making with them was, *"We will do everything the LORD has said; we will obey."*[23] They accepted the terms of this covenant. But we know that Israel doesn't fulfill what they agreed to. They turned their backs on God and they chased after other idols in their lives.

God saw their unfaithfulness to what they claimed they would live out. In Jeremiah 11:10 God says, *"They have returned to the sins of their forefathers, who refused to listen to my words. They have followed other gods to serve them. Both the house of Israel and the house of Judah have <u>broken the covenant</u> I made with their forefathers."* Israel & Judah broke their part of the agreement. We see that God is not happy that they chose to break the agreement that they had made with Him. No one would be happy if someone was unfaithful to them in an agreement made. Jeremiah goes on and paints a vivid picture for us to see God's displeasure. In Jeremiah 18, God tells Jeremiah to go to the house of the potter. So Jeremiah goes to the potter's house and he sees the potter at the wheel forming a pot out of clay. The potter takes great care in making the pot. The message is that the people of Israel are the clay and God is the potter shaping them as He sees fit. It is important for us to see that Israel is the pot. In the very next chapter, Jeremiah 19, God has Jeremiah take the clay pot and smash it.

Israel's disobedience of their covenant to God left them broken. Israel is sent into exile where they are prisoners of other countries for 70 years. All seemed lost.

But in the midst of the exile, they get some good news. One of the most well known verses is Jeremiah 29:11, *"'For I know the plans I have for you,' declares the Lord, 'plans to prosper you and*

> **God kept His part of the covenant perfectly, but man couldn't keep their part.**

not to harm you, plans to give you hope and a future." Even though they were unfaithful to God and broke His covenant, which resulted in exile, there was still a promise of something good. What can be good when their relationship with God has been severed? What good can be promised? God promises restoration to Him. God knows the old covenant can't work because no one can live up to their part of the agreement. God kept His part of the covenant perfectly, but man couldn't keep their part. So God promises a new covenant; a new agreement between God and man. In Jeremiah 31:31-33 we see this new covenant that God promises to give in the future, *"'The time is coming,' declares the Lord, 'when I will make a new covenant with the house of Israel and with the house of Judah. It will not be like the covenant I made with their forefathers when I took them by the hand to lead them out of Egypt, because they broke my covenant, though I was a husband to them,' declares the Lord. 'This is the covenant I will make with the house of Israel after that time,' declares the Lord. 'I will put my law in their minds and write it on their hearts. I will be their God, and they will be my people."* God needed to establish a new covenant (or agreement) because if one party breaks the covenant…the covenant is completely broken. So He sent Jesus into the world to usher in the new covenant, a new agreement with man.

New Covenant with God

Marriage is an example of a covenant relationship. Both husband and wife agree to love, honor, and be faithful to each other as long as they both shall live. This marriage relationship is completely different than all of our other relationships. Your spouse is your helpmate for life. We may have good neighbors and good friends but we don't have that same level of commitment with them as we do with our spouse. We don't have a covenant relationship with our neighbors. We will help them if we can…and who knows; in the future we may move far away from them and get new neighbors. But in our covenant walk with our spouse, we are committed to them for life.

Too often we treat our relationship with God like He is a good friend or neighbor. We treat him like any other relationship that we have. But our relationship with God should be a covenant relationship. Our baptism is like our wedding day to God. When we are baptized it is like we say to God, "I love you, and at this moment I vow to follow and be faithful to you for the rest of my life."

Your marriage will only be good if both people live up to their part of the covenant agreement. If your spouse is only looking out for their own best interest, the marriage will not be a good one. My wife, Janelle, and I just made this covenant vow to one another not too long ago. I vowed to spend the rest of my life with her…to love her, cherish her, and put no one ahead of her, and to be faithful to her as long as we both shall live. What if in our counseling session, as she is sitting beside me, I made this comment to the preacher marrying us, "What is the least amount I need to do, and yet still be married to her? Do I have to show an interest in the things she does? Do I have to provide for her? Do I have to put her number one in my life all the time?" How do you think that would go over with Janelle? Not good, and understandably so. I still expect her to meet her marital obligations to me, and be my helpmate...and yet in return, I am asking what the least amount is that I can do for her? I want to be married, but I don't want to give up anything? I want all that she has to offer me, but I can't possibly make the same sacrifices back to her? I am basically saying, "I only want the blessings of married life, but I don't want to put in all the work." Would you want to be in that kind of a relationship with this type of person? No way!

Unfortunately, that is how most of us enter into our relationship with Jesus. We want the eternal life that He has to offer; we want His love, His peace, His guidance, His protection, and we want His provisions... we want all the blessings of God, but we don't want to do much of anything in return. We want and expect God to keep His part of the agreement, while we are very passive about living out our part? We think to ourselves, "God is merciful, so I don't need to live out my part." That is a lie from the devil. We have a tendency to think we can be the same unchanged people we have always been, and that we don't need to change anything because Jesus will forgive us anyway. God is merciful, but that does not mean we keep on living a selfish and sinful life. He died to forgive our sins, not to allow us to keep on living for ourselves.

I'm not questioning whether you have a relationship with Jesus or not. I believe you all do or you would not be reading this book. But the question is; do you have a covenant relationship with Him? Or is He like the neighbor next door you contact only when you need help? God demands more than that. Our relationship with

> **We want the covenant blessings, but we don't want to live out our part of the covenant agreement.**

God should be like the relationship you have with your spouse. It is a daily walk, in good times and in the times where it becomes a real sacrifice to fulfill your covenant obligations. Just like in your marriage, it is not always easy to live for God, but it is so worth it. Stop and think about who is getting the better end of the deal in our relationship with God. If you look at all that God offers in His part of the covenant, compared to what we need to do in our part of the covenant...we are really getting a great deal. We have the power of the Holy Spirit in our earthly lives, and we have eternal life waiting for us. God treats us like His favorite son or daughter. You are the apple of his eye.

Just like the Israelites, we can't live up to the covenant by ourselves. No matter how hard we try, we fall short of following the new covenant stipulations. For those who have given our lives over to him—our desire is to live for him. But there are times we do fail. Romans 3:23, *"for all have sinned and fall short of the glory of God."* Jesus' blood covers our sins if we are in a covenant relationship with him. We need to see that a covenant relationship is not a relationship that we can be committed to one week and the next week not be committed to. A covenant relationship is one that is a committed relationship for life. If you want the blessings that come with the covenant relationship with God, you have to live out your end of the covenant relationship.

Some people don't follow God because they find it hard to leave the life they want to live. They don't want to forgive other people when they have been hurt, they don't want to give God the money He desires, and they don't want to watch what they say. The list goes on and on of the ways we don't want to live out what we agreed to at baptism. Some people choose not to be a part of this covenant relationship with God because they want to chase after the things that make them happy. They even deceive themselves thinking, "God wants me to be happy. Therefore God doesn't mind me doing these things to gain my happiness." So they make it their goal to pursue happiness. We are not to pursue happiness. We pursue God, and He will give us the joy and the happiness and blessings that are within His plan. The happiness that we chase after in this world does not last, but the joy found in a covenant relationship with Christ lasts forever.

We have many, many relationships in our lives, but only a few are covenant relationships. We have many relationships where we haven't committed or don't need to commit to anything. We may have a relationship with God—but we aren't committed to him. Our relationship with God can be like that spoiled rotten neighbor who borrows everything and asks you to do things for them, but they never want to do anything for you. Is your relationship with God completely one sided? If so, you

> *We are not to pursue happiness. We pursue God, and He will give us the joy and the happiness and blessings that are within His plan.*

are not in a covenant relationship with Him.

In my covenant relationship with my wife, I don't have to worry about her leaving me. She is committed to the Lord and to me. I don't have to fear doing one thing wrong, or doing too many things wrong and worry about her leaving. In the marriage covenant, I do mess up. But I confess my wrong, and ask for her forgiveness. The covenant is not broken each time one of us messes up. It is the same way with God. In our covenant walk with him, we will mess up, we will sin. But that does not mean the covenant is broken. I need to confess my sin and ask Him to forgive me. I don't have to live in constant fear of whether or not I am going to heaven. Romans 8:1 says, *"Therefore, there is now no condemnation for those who are in Christ Jesus."* If I am committed to walking with Him, He is committed to washing away my sins, and allowing me to live with Him forever. Friend, there is no better place to be than in a covenant relationship with God through the blood of Jesus Christ!

chapter 8

Money

M oney is always a difficult subject to talk about.
People do not like to be told how to spend their
money. Hopefully as we go through this chapter, you
will see that faithfulness in finances is something that
God is really concerned about.

This is not my money.

Let me share with you three scriptures that give
evidence that we do not own our money. Psalm 24:1,
*"The earth is the LORD's, and everything in it, the world,
and all who live in it;"* Haggai 2:8, *"'The silver is mine
and the gold is mine,' declares the LORD Almighty."*
Deuteronomy 8:18 says, *"But remember the LORD your
God, for it is he who gives you the ability to produce
wealth..."* In these passages, God makes it clear that
the gold and silver are His and the world is His. He
also makes it clear that He even gives you the ability
to produce wealth. God is telling us a simple fact that
we <u>must</u> understand: God owns it all. What we have is
not partly God's and partly ours. It is all God's! He has
given it to us to use for a short while. If we understand
this principle it changes our approach to our finances. If
God is the owner, I must be the manager. I am supposed
to be the faithful manager to allocate his money wisely.
I use the assets that I have been entrusted with for my
owners benefit. Do we see ourselves as the owners

of what we have or as managers of God's money? A manager carries no sense of entitlement to the assets of the manager. We divvy out <u>His</u> money in the way that <u>He</u> wants us to…not in the way we would like to. The money manager listens to the owner of the money. If you had someone managing your money, you wouldn't want them spending it however they wanted to. They spend it according to how you want them to.[24]

If we believe everything we have is ours, of course we are going to find it a struggle to give to God's work. We will think to ourselves, "I'm not going to give up my hard earned money; I am going to use <u>my</u> money to better <u>myself</u>." Jesus gives us a very strong warning for his money managers (you). He says in Luke 16:10-11, *"Whoever can be trusted with very little can also be trusted with much, and whoever is dishonest with very little will also be dishonest with much. So if you have not been trustworthy in handling worldly wealth, who will trust you with true riches?"* Jesus trusts us with His money here on earth, and if we can't manage these earthly treasures for a short time…why would He give us His true heavenly riches permanently?

When you see God as the owner of all that we have, it is easier to see God's complaint to His people in Malachi 3, which we will look at in more depth in a little while. In Malachi 3 God says we are robbing him. We are robbing him of our "tithes and offerings." Israel owed God a tithe which was 10% and then on top of that, they are to bring freewill offerings. Israel didn't even bring their

> **If we believe everything we have is ours, of course we are going to find it a struggle to give to God's work.**

tithe, let alone any offering in addition to that. God was basically saying you are not managing my money well, you are robbing me. The problem is that so many people today are robbing the Lord in the same way. I believe lots of people rob God because they haven't got a hold of this principle. God is the owner and we are just the managers. What must the owner think, when his money manager is living in a huge house, driving fancy cars, wearing expensive clothes or jewelry? Won't the owner call the manager to give an account for squandering <u>His</u> money? God will also call us to account on how we spend <u>His</u> money.

Give God the Tithe

I saw a cartoon one time that made me laugh hysterically, and yet at the same time mourn the truth that the cartoon showed. The cartoon was a picture of a man being baptized. His entire body was completely immersed under the water, except his hand which was reaching out of the water with his wallet. He wasn't going to baptize his wallet. He was surrendering his entire life to God, except for his finances. How true that is with most Christians today. God has a plan for His followers when it comes to finances. Let's start in Malachi 3.

> [6] *"I the LORD do not change. So you, O descendants of Jacob, are not destroyed. [7] Ever since the time of your forefathers you have turned away from my decrees and have not kept them. Return to me, and I will return to you," says the LORD Almighty. "But you ask, 'How are we to return?' [8] "Will a man rob*

God? Yet you rob me. "But you ask, 'How do we rob you?' "In tithes and offerings. [9] You are under a curse-the whole nation of you-because you are robbing me. [10] Bring the whole tithe into the storehouse, that there may be food in my house. Test me in this," says the LORD Almighty, "and see if I will not throw open the floodgates of heaven and pour out so much blessing that you will not have room enough for it. [11] I will prevent pests from devouring your crops, and the vines in your fields will not cast their fruit," says the LORD Almighty. [12] "Then all the nations will call you blessed, for yours will be a delightful land," says the LORD Almighty.

God brings a serious charge against his people: that they are robbing him because they are not giving their tithes to Him. Again this is clearly spelled out in the law that they are required to give tithes back to God. It wasn't optional—it was in the law. Maybe there is some question to what a tithe is? A tithe means 10%. It is giving 10% of your money back to God. He gave you all that you have, He just asks for a small portion of it back.

Verse 10 says, "*'Bring the whole tithe into the storehouse, that there may be food in my house. Test me in this,' says the Lord Almighty, 'and see if I will not throw open the floodgates of heaven and pour out so much blessing that you will not have room enough for it.'*" How much were they supposed to bring to God?

Bring the whole tithe. Bring the full 10%. People were giving to the Lord, but they were not giving what they needed to be giving. It is the same way today. Tithing is not a way of life for God's people. The Barna Research Group reported that tithing among born again Christians has taken a huge drop. In the year 2000—12% of Christians tithed (Just over 1 out of 10 Christians gave a tithe). In 2001—it actually went up to 14%. But in 2002—it dropped to only 6% of born again Christians tithing.[26] In two years, the number of Christians tithing was cut in half. It wasn't very high to begin with. This is a sad fact for the church— 6 out of 100 Christians tithe to the Lord. There are only 6% of Christians who are handling their money the way that God would have them handle it. That statistic continues to go down each year as people are less and less committed to the Lord and more and more focused on accumulating worldly wealth for themselves. James 4:4 says, *"You adulterous people, don't you know that friendship with the world is hatred toward God? Anyone who chooses to be a friend of the world becomes an enemy of God."* Make sure you are not an enemy of God. Serve God, not the things of this world.

I saw a story this week, and I didn't know whether to laugh or to cry: For years we lived in a small town with one bank and three churches. Early one Monday morning, the bank called all three churches with the same request, "Could you bring in Sunday's collection right away? We're out of one-dollar bills."[27]

Can we just step back and catch a glimpse of how God's kingdom can expand if we would all give our resources to Him? But we somehow convince ourselves, "I can't afford it." I have other things I need my money for. God doesn't demand we give everything back to him, just a tithe. We need to take a serious look at how we are spending our money. God, in this passage, says we are robbing him. Ouch! Doesn't that have a hollowing sound to it? Christians are robbing God. They keep money that is God's. When we owe somebody $200 we pay them back. But when we owe God that, for some reason we keep it or just pay Him far less than we should. We hoard our money from God and He is the one who gave it to us in the first place. I challenge every Christian to stop robbing God and give him what He deserves.

I always tell people, "Don't let your lifestyle dictate your giving, instead let your giving dictate your lifestyle." We usually let our lifestyle dictate what we give. We go out during the week and buy $100 worth of tickets and food at Six Flags and then all we have left on Sunday is $10 to drop in the offering plate for God. We spend $50 to go out to eat, watch a movie and buy candy—then on Sunday we put $10 in the offering plate. We go on fancy vacations and pay $1,000, and when Sunday comes around we put $10 in the offering plate. You can substitute a lot of things and give them priority over what we give to God. I am not saying these things are wrong. We need to take vacations and have a night out in town, but not at the expense of the Kingdom of God.

If we would change our priorities and make our giving dictate our lifestyle, we would see a big change.

"Don't let your lifestyle dictate your giving, instead let your giving dictate your lifestyle."

Immediately when we receive a check, we should write a check for 10% to the church. Then whatever we have left we can spend however we would like to spend it.

This teaches us to buy only the things that we need. As Christians, we need to learn to live on 90% of our money that is blessed by God, instead of living on 98% of our money that is not blessed. I challenge you to adapt your life around your giving. Remember, giving is an act of worship to God.

I hear people making up other ways to justify not giving a tithe. "I will do things for the church as my tithe (teach Sunday school, lead Youth group, be on the church board). I will work for the church and the older generation will tithe for the church." I am wondering which chapter of the Bible I missed. Did God give us a choice? Either work in the church or tithe to the church. Pick one! NO!! Scripture teaches us to do both— to do work in the church and to tithe. Some people think that pastors preach about tithing so they can get paid. But let me tell you, the pastor gets paid whether you tithe or not. Pastors should preach about tithing to help their congregation surrender to God's Will. This Malachi passage is not about paying your pastor, it is about people being obedient to God.

The second half of verse 10 says, *"'Test me in this,' says the Lord Almighty, 'and see if I will not throw open the floodgates of heaven and pour out so much blessing that you will not have room enough for it.'"* God says bring the whole tithe...test Him in this. The only place that God says to test Him is in the area of our finances. In other areas, God says do not test the Lord your God. For some reason it is very hard to trust that God will provide for us if we give more to Him. But God says He wants to bring down a blessing upon you. He didn't say He would sprinkle down blessings on you when you tithe, He said He would open up the floodgates of heaven—you would not have room enough for all the blessings in your life. That isn't to say that there won't be struggles. "I will give a tithe and then all of a sudden I will win the lottery." There may be some struggles, but God will see you through. I have heard some great testimonies from people about what happened when they started tithing. They would get checks in the mail that they did not realize they would be getting, or they would get checks for more than they thought the amount would be. I love to see how God brings it back to you. You give it to Him, He brings it back in other ways; either in financial blessings, spiritual blessings, or relational blessings. You can't out give God. It is impossible. So test God in your finances and see what happens.

Sometimes we look for loopholes in scripture so we don't have to tithe. Some may say, "Tithing was under the old covenant, not the new covenant." Which is true, but Jesus often demands even more in the new covenant. Jesus says when you look at a girl lustfully you commit adultery in your heart.[29] Or if you are angry at your brother, you commit murder.[30] God desires more from us than just following the written law. I know there are many people who give 20 to 30 percent of their income to the Lord. They give out of their love. Don't try to find a loophole in giving.

> *He didn't say He would sprinkle down blessings on you when you tithe, He said He would open up the floodgates of heaven— you would not have room enough for all the blessings in your life.*

What is our attitude when it comes to giving? Here is an interesting story about a certain group's heart to give to God.

There were a few people who went on a mission trip to Eastern Europe. When they came back, they were really impressed with the dedication of the Christians in Romania. Christians there don't have very much, but they believe they should tithe. They think tithing is God's standard. But the government of Romania is repressive, and they only allow the people to give 2.5 percent of their income to charitable organizations. They're trying to minimize the opportunity for any anti-government organization. So Romanians are searching for loopholes in the law, so that they can give 10 percent.[33]

That should be a wake-up call for Christians in the wealthiest nations of the world. Often we do the opposite…we are looking for loopholes in the Scripture to avoid giving the tithe. Let's not dodge the tithe anymore. Let's not look for loopholes to get out of it. Let's seriously look for ways we can get ourselves to tithe.

Can any of you say God just doesn't want me to give 10% of my money back to him…He is pleased enough with 3%? We need to stop and evaluate, "Is God pleased with the sacrifice I am making for Him in my life?" Maybe as you are reading this today, you are being nudged by the Spirit, "I know I need to start tithing, but how? I can't." Whenever you receive your paycheck, turn around and write 10% of whatever that check was back to God. Trust him to provide the money that you need. When you start doing that, you will have to stop spending money in other areas of your lives. You may have to cut down the number of clothes you buy, or cut down the number of times you go out to eat. You may have to cancel your cable bill or your cell phone. You may have to stop buying all those cute little knick knacks that you put all around the house. There are many ways that we can afford to tithe if we wanted to tithe bad enough. There may be big sacrifices that you have to make, but they will all be worth it because it will strengthen your relationship with God.

> *There are many ways that we can afford to tithe if we wanted to tithe bad enough.*

Storing up for yourself

There is a story told about a man who opens a newspaper and discovers the date on the newspaper is six months in advance of the time he lives. He begins to read through the newspaper, and he discovers stories about events that have not yet taken place. He turns to the sports page, and there are scores of games not yet played. He turns to the financial page and discovers a report of the rise and fall of different stocks and bonds. He realizes this can make him a wealthy man. A few large bets on an underdog team he knows will win will make him wealthy. Investments in stocks that are now low but will get high can fatten his portfolio. He is delighted. He turns the page and comes to the obituary column and sees his picture and story. Everything changes. The knowledge of his death changes his view about his wealth.

In Luke 12 it says,

¹³Someone in the crowd said to him, "Teacher, tell my brother to divide the inheritance with me." ¹⁴Jesus replied, "Man, who appointed me a judge or an arbiter between you?" ¹⁵Then he said to them, "Watch out! Be on your guard against all kinds of greed; a man's life does not consist in the abundance of his possessions." ¹⁶And he told them this parable: "The ground of a certain rich man produced a good crop. ¹⁷He thought to himself, 'What shall I do? I have no place to store my crops.' ¹⁸"Then he said, 'This is what I'll do. I will tear down my barns and build bigger ones, and there I will store all my grain and my goods. ¹⁹And I'll say to myself, "You have plenty of good things laid up for many years. Take life easy; eat, drink and be merry." ' ²⁰"But God said to him, 'You fool! This very night your life will be demanded from you. Then who will get what you have prepared for yourself?' ²¹"This is how it will be with anyone who stores up things for himself but is not rich toward God."

The main issue in this parable is not the wealth. It is on one's attitude towards the wealth. The man in this story happens to have a fruitful harvest, and he must decide what to do with the overflow. He did not acquire his harvest immorally; he just had a good year. He was not wrong for having a lot of money, he was wrong because of how he used his money. We all are in the same boat. God has given to us generously and now we must see that we do not hoard it all for ourselves. Our wealth opens up choices for us that allow us to pursue our own interest or to further God's kingdom.

Many people say that this parable is not for them, because they are not wealthy. But this parable is not exclusively for the wealthy. It is for everybody. The underlying question is: What do you do with the money that you have? Christians have more money than they think. Sometimes we just waste money. I think about all the things that I have spent money on over the years and I regret many of my purchases. I buy something and use it for a couple months and then forget about it. I have a bunch of CD's that I hardly ever listen to anymore. Can you imagine what the Lord could have done with all of the money that I spent selfishly on myself? Now multiply that by hundreds of millions of Christians. Many lives could have been touched by the gospel instead of us purchasing the stuff that we really don't need. I am now willing to watch my purchases a lot closer now. Jesus warns us in Luke 12:15, *"Then he said to them, 'Watch out! Be on your guard against all kinds of greed; a man's life does not consist in the abundance of his possessions.'"* We are all susceptible to the love of money and stuff. We sometimes place a higher priority on these things, than we do on giving it to God. The world wants your money…but so does God. God wants to be Lord of your life, which includes your finances.

The man in this parable is an example of greed. He had a great crop and verse 18 tells us what he did with it. *"Then he said, 'This is what I'll do. I will tear down my barns and build bigger ones, and there I will store all my grain and my goods.'"* This man didn't even think about giving up his money. It was his and he was going to keep it. The man didn't even realize how he received what he had. All that he had was a blessing from God. It is God that blessed this man's harvest. Instead of this man giving to the poor and hurting, he took what he had and he stored it for his own future. There are people without food, without housing, without medical care… and what does this man do? He stores some more back for himself. I find myself outraged towards the man when I think about what he is doing. Then at a second glance, this looks a lot like our retirement plans. We store away for ourselves for later in life, when there are people that are in serious need today. Am I saying that saving for retirement is wrong? I believe it is wrong if you are not tithing to God, but instead you are taking what belongs to Him and storing up things for yourself. You are doing what this man is doing. There is a need for that grain in the kingdom of God, but instead of giving it up, you store up for your own future. Retirement plans are not wrong if you are sensitive to God's leading on your finances.

We need to take this seriously. God dealt with this man. He had him killed that very night and called him a fool for only thinking of himself.

> **There are people without food, without housing, without medical care… and what does this man do? He stores some more back for himself.**

Jesus says in verse 21, "This is how it will be with anyone who stores up things for himself but is not rich toward

God." God is warning us that He will not let this greed go unpunished. We need to be more concerned about the needs around us, and less focused on getting the toys that we want.

My heart goes with the money.

Many Christians are holding on to this world like it is all they have. They feel that way because that is where they have put their treasure. Each day, they are one day closer to losing all their treasures that they have worked so hard for. Luke 12:34 says, *"For where your treasure is, there your heart will be also."* How true. Where you put your treasure; that is where your heart will be.

> Suppose you know very little about cars, but you make a big investment in General Motors. You buy lots of stock. Suddenly you develop an interest in GM. You check the financial pages. You see a magazine article about GM, which you stop and read, when a month ago you wouldn't have. You develop more of an interest in something if you invest money into it.[33]

I find this true in my life as well. I am a big supporter of the organization Gospel for Asia. Before I supported them, I didn't care very much about news that I heard about in India. Now, if I hear any news that happens in India—I really take notice and listen to what is happening. I often ask myself, "How does this news affect those who are planting churches in that region?"

My heart is in God's work in India.

If you want to know where your treasure lies... look at your check book or credit card statements. Where is the money God gave you going? We often think we own our possessions, but the truth of the matter is that our possessions own us. We work like dogs to afford the things that we want, and all the things we want capture the attention of our hearts. Henry Ford worked his whole life and became a very rich man as he sold his Ford vehicles. He must have had it all, right? Well, Henry Ford says, "I was happier when I was doing a mechanic's job."[34] He was happier as a mechanic than a rich business man. Chasing after the things of this world stole his joy.

Invest in the right things.

We all invest our money in different things, but have we really stopped to think about the investments that we are making? Here is a story that should get us thinking about the bigger picture of how we should view our investments.

> Imagine you're alive at the end of the Civil War. You're living in the South, but you are a Northerner. You plan to move home as soon as the war is over. While in the South, you've accumulated a lot of Confederate currency. Now, suppose you know for a fact that the North is going to win the war and the end is imminent. What will you do with your Confederate money? If you are smart, there's only one answer. You should immediately cash in

your Confederate currency for U.S. currency—the only money that will have value once the war is over. Keep only enough Confederate currency to meet your short-term needs.[35]

Well, as Christians we live for a brief time in a world that is not our own. We can accumulate a lot of money & possessions. But we need to see that we are soon going to be going home—where our money & possessions will do us no good. Our money is worthless in heaven. To accumulate vast amounts of earthly treasures that you can't possibly hold on to is like stockpiling Confederate money even though you know it's about to become worthless.

Our money is worthless in heaven.

Matthew 6:19-21 says, *"Do not store up for yourselves treasures on earth, where moth and rust destroy, and where thieves break in and steal. But store up for yourselves treasures in heaven, where moth and rust do not destroy, and where thieves do not break in and steal. For where your treasure is, there your heart will be also."* People think that Jesus was against us storing up treasures for ourselves. No, He's all for it. In fact, he commands it. Jesus has a treasure mentality. He just says, store up the right treasures. Stop storing up treasures in the wrong places and start storing them in the right places. If you store up treasures here in this world…it is only temporary. Your treasures will eventually break, get lost, be stolen, or you will depart from them at death. As the saying goes, "You have never seen a hearse with a U-haul", because you can't take it with you. "John D Rockefeller was one of the wealthiest men who ever lived. After he died, someone asked his accountant, 'How much money did John leave?' His accountant replied, 'He left all of it.'"[36]

As I thought about this concept, I came to the conclusion that, if you store up treasures here on earth—you lose twice. First, you lose because these things don't last. Secondly, you lose in the next life. 1 Corinthians 3:12-15, says, *"If any man builds on this foundation using gold, silver, costly stones, wood, hay or straw, his work will be shown for what it is, because the Day will bring it to light. It will be revealed with fire, and the fire will test the quality of each man's work. If what he has built survives, he will receive his reward. If it is burned up, he will suffer loss; he himself will be saved, but only as one escaping through the flames."* In this life we build on the foundation of Jesus Christ. Some build by using costly stones—they invest time and money into God's kingdom. At the end of time, these things remain after God's purifying fire. Others build by using wood, hay or straw—they do things in this life that don't further God's kingdom. And when they stand before God, his purifying fire will reveal that they lived for the temporary.

There is going to be a day when people are going to see…"I made bad investments in my life. I invested my money here and not in heaven." Luckily, as a believer this passage tells me that even though you suffer loss, you yourself will be saved. But there is a way that you can have something lasting. It's clear you can't take it with you when you go, but you can send it ahead of you. You send it ahead by investing in the things that further God's kingdom. Missionary Jim Elliot said, "He is no fool who gives up what he cannot keep to gain that which he cannot lose."[37] If you give to the Lord's work, there is no way anyone can take away your reward. That is a sure investment! That is not the case with the material possessions we accumulate here. The stock market falls, things are stolen, things break, things are misplaced and lost. Your treasure is never secure. Financial planners will tell you to think about how your investment will pay off in thirty or thirty five years. The Bible tells us to think well beyond that. Think about how your investments will still be paying off millions of years from now.[38]

You read about the people in the Bible who forsook their treasures in this world to live for the next. Zacchaeus gave away half his wealth to the poor and repaid anyone he

> *There is going to be a day when people are going to see..."I made bad investments in my life. I invested my money here and not in heaven."*

cheated 4 times the amount. The Ephesians proved their sincerity by burning their magic books, which would be equivalent to millions of dollars today. And yet there were others like the Rich young ruler who could not give up his money to follow Jesus—because it meant too much to him. Luke 16:13 says, *"No servant can serve two masters. Either he will hate the one and love the other, or he will be devoted to the one and despise the other. You cannot serve both God and money."* You must choose today saying, "Am I serving God or am I serving my money by letting it control my happiness?"

Chapter 9

Forgiving Others

There was an old TV show called "Amos and Andy". In one episode, Andy was angry because there was a big man who would continually slap Andy across the chest every time they met. Andy finally had enough of it. He told Amos, "I'm going to get revenge. I will put a stick of dynamite in my vest pocket. The next time he slaps me on the chest he's going to get his hand blown off."[39]

Does anybody see the problem in that? Andy wasn't thinking about the fact that the dynamite would kill him. The point is, revenge may hurt the other person but it always takes a toll on you as well. It is always hard on the heart.

Always forgive

Over and over again Jesus forgave people for doing wrong to Him. Jesus did not forgive a couple times here and there. It was part of his lifestyle. He forgave everyone, whether they asked him to forgive them or not. How many times are we to forgive someone who sins against us? Jesus was asked that question in Matthew 18:21-22. *"Then Peter came to Jesus and asked, 'Lord, how many times shall I forgive my brother when he sins against me? Up to seven times?' Jesus answered, 'I tell you, not seven times, but seventy seven times.'"*

The tradition of the rabbis was to forgive someone

three times. But Peter realized that Jesus was really emphasizing forgiveness— he knew that three times was not enough. So Peter thought he would be generous and forgive someone seven times. Peter had the idea that he needed to forgive more, but he still didn't grasp the idea. He put a limit on the number of times he had to forgive. Jesus answers Peter by saying there is no limit to forgiveness. He said not seven times but seventy-seven times. Jesus does not literally mean to forgive seventy-seven times. He doesn't mean, "I am going to start counting and once you reach the 78th time I am not going to forgive you anymore." Jesus exaggerates on what Peter said to make a point. Peter used the number seven, which is a number to signify completeness. Jesus multiplies it significantly to drive the point home that we are to forgive our brothers each and every time they sin against us. Jesus does not want his followers to count how many times people hurt us, but He wants us to be in a mindset that is always open for forgiveness and reconciliation.

In a position that we must forgive

Jesus goes on in Matthew 18 to show the reason why we must be willing to forgive.

> 23 "Therefore, the kingdom of heaven is like a king who wanted to settle accounts with his servants. 24As he began the settlement, a man who owed him ten thousand talents was brought to him. 25Since he was not able to pay, the master ordered that he and his wife and his children and all that he had be sold to repay the debt. 26"The servant fell on his

knees before him. 'Be patient with me,' he begged, 'and I will pay back everything.' ²⁷*The servant's master took pity on him, canceled the debt and let him go.* ²⁸*"But when that servant went out, he found one of his fellow servants who owed him a hundred denarii. He grabbed him and began to choke him. 'Pay back what you owe me!' he demanded.* ²⁹*"His fellow servant fell to his knees and begged him, 'Be patient with me, and I will pay you back.'* ³⁰*"But he refused. Instead, he went off and had the man thrown into prison until he could pay the debt.* ³¹*When the other servants saw what had happened, they were greatly distressed and went and told their master everything that had happened.* ³²*"Then the master called the servant in. 'You wicked servant,' he said, 'I canceled all that debt of yours because you begged me to.* ³³*Shouldn't you have had mercy on your fellow servant just as I had on you?'* ³⁴*In anger his master turned him over to the jailers to be tortured, until he should pay back all he owed.* ³⁵*"This is how my heavenly Father will treat each of you unless you forgive your brother from your heart."*

This man owed the king ten thousand talents. A talent was the largest measurement of money in that day, just like our dollar is the largest today, compared to a quarter, dime, nickel and penny. Ten thousand was said to be the biggest number in ancient Greek vocabulary, so the number ten thousand plus the term talents together represented the biggest debt that you can imagine. It was a number to show the human impossibility of paying off such a debt. This amount was more than a servant could ever expect to make in many, many life times. Try and think of the biggest amount of money possible. We could say one hundred zillion dollars. There is no way anybody can make this amount of money in their lifetime. Yet this servant said, "Be patient with me, I will pay it back." The king knew the man would never be able to pay off such a big debt, but the king forgave this man's huge debt out of compassion for this man. He did not forgive him because he was expecting something in return. He didn't say, "I will forgive you, but first you have to promise that you will…" He saw that the man was not able to pay; in fact there is no way that anybody could have paid off such a debt.

So this man left the king's presence being totally cleared of his large debt. Sometime later the servant met a fellow servant who owed him money. He demanded the servant to pay it back to him. This second servant used the same exact words the first servant used, "Be patient with me, I will pay you back." There is a good chance that this man actually could have paid back his debt in time. But obviously the first servant did not think twice about the forgiveness that he had just received. All he thought

> *…if we forget about the huge debt that we have just been forgiven of…the second debt will obviously look pretty big.*

about and focused on was the debt that someone owed him. It was far less money than the debt his master canceled for him. The money this man owed is about 1 millionth of the debt that was canceled. So when we look at this small debt compared to the one he was forgiven of…it is truly a small debt. However, if we forget about the huge debt that we have just been forgiven of…the second debt will obviously look pretty big. This second servant owed a lot of money to the first servant. He owed this servant 100 denarii. A denarius was a Roman silver coin that was worth about 16 cents. 16 cents does not sound like much to us, but that is a whole day's wage. So, 100 denarii is 100 days of wages. It is hard to let go of over three months of wages. This man definitely had problems forgiving. Let's face it, sometimes forgiving is really hard to do. There may be people in your life that you find hard to forgive because they may owe you a lot. You look at your situation and say you didn't get what you deserved. It is crystal clear that someone owes you something: Money, respect, an apology. They hurt you so badly; how can you forgive them?

Think about how you would feel if you were in this king's situation. Let's say you owned a house and you sold it to this poor couple with kids who were down on their luck. This couple could not get a loan, so you just told them to pay you as they earned the money. Several months later they have not paid you a single penny for the house. You tell them you have no choice but to get the police involved, unless they can pay what they owe you. They beg you not to do that. They remind you of their situation and ask for more time to be able to pay. You knew they would never be able to pay you back, but you forgive them. And not only do you give them more time to pay you back, instead you give them the house for free. You canceled the debt they had. You gave them something that they did not deserve— this beautiful eight hundred thousand dollar house. Then, a week later you hear that this couple is suing a single mother for $300. This single mother could not pay back the money in which she borrowed to provide groceries for her family. This mother was having a tough time putting food on the table for her family. The mother begged them for more time, saying, "I will be able to get it to you next week when I get paid." But the couple refused and called the police. Wouldn't you be angry with this couple for not showing mercy to this person, just as you showed mercy to them?

We can see that this parable demonstrated two extremes. One person is showing mercy for a debt that is so large he could never pay it off and the other person is not showing any mercy for a much smaller debt. The meaning of this parable is clear. The king is God and we have a debt of sin that is so large that we have no hopes of ever paying it back. But God, in his compassion, has canceled the debt. He sent his Son to die on the cross to cancel the debt. This debt of sin could not be paid off any other way. We could work 10 lifetimes and still not even come close to paying off the huge debt we owe God. Since God has paid this price for us, we are not to go and find others who owe us a debt that is far less and make them pay. You are totally forgiven and He wants you to go share forgiveness with others. When we look at other people's debt to us, it may seem like a huge debt that they owe us because we compare it to our human standards. But if we compare the debt they owe us with the debt that we owed God before He cancelled it...we will see that we must forgive or we are exactly like the unmerciful servant in this parable. This man was shown love and compassion, yet he went out and showed others hate and unconcern.

The king at the end of this parable took back his mercy because this man didn't show mercy to others. Jesus says in Matthew 6:14-15, *"For if you forgive men when they sin against you, your heavenly Father will also forgive you. But if you do not forgive men their sins, your Father will not forgive your sins."* Jesus commands us to forgive others the same way that He has forgiven us.

> **We could work 10 lifetimes and still not even come close to paying off the huge debt we owe God.**

Love your enemies

In Matthew 5 it goes on to say we should not just forgive our friends or acquaintances when they hurt us, but we should even love our enemies.

> [38] *"You have heard that it was said, 'Eye for eye, and tooth for tooth.'* [39] *But I tell you, Do not resist an evil person. If someone strikes you on the right cheek, turn to him the other also.* [40] *And if someone wants to sue you and take your tunic, let him have your cloak as well.* [41] *If someone forces you to go one mile, go with him two miles.* [42] *Give to the one who asks you, and do not turn away from the one who wants to borrow from you.* [43] *"You have heard that it was said, 'Love your neighbor and hate your enemy.'*

⁴⁴But I tell you: Love your enemies and pray for those who persecute you, ⁴⁵that you may be sons of your Father in heaven. He causes his sun to rise on the evil and the good, and sends rain on the righteous and the unrighteous. ⁴⁶If you love those who love you, what reward will you get? Are not even the tax collectors doing that? ⁴⁷And if you greet only your brothers, what are you doing more than others? Do not even pagans do that? ⁴⁸Be perfect, therefore, as your heavenly Father is perfect.

We need to learn to endure a little extra for Jesus. Usually when our rights have been violated, we want people to know about it. When someone has treated us wrong—we want to get back at them. "They hurt me, now I am going to hurt them."

There is a story of a mother who ran into the bedroom when she heard her seven-year-old son scream. She found his two-year-old sister pulling his hair. She gently released the little girl's grip and said comfortingly to the boy, "There, there. She didn't mean it. She doesn't know that hurts." He nodded his acknowledgement, and the mother left the room. As she started down the hall the little girl screamed. Rushing back in, she

asked, "What happened?" The little
boy replied, "She knows now."[40]

There is just something about our nature that we
want to get even. If you do something to me—you better
not go to sleep because I will get you back. We think it
is our right to get back at people for the pain they have
caused us. But Jesus says that his followers should not
seek revenge for being hurt. Jesus says in verse 38, *"You
have heard that it was said, 'Eye for eye, and tooth for
tooth.'"* In the Old Testament it was your right to inflict
the exact punishment back upon them as they did to you.
The people of that day used this law as a way of hurting
others, but that wasn't the intent of the law. The law
was not set in place to seek revenge and hurt others; the
law was given to bring justice. Breaking the law has
consequences, but personal revenge is wrong. Look at
the heart of the law. The law was given to bring harmony
in relationships, not to cause problems. In this day, there
wasn't much said about forgiveness—it was "you did
this to me, I will do this right back to you." But Jesus
goes on to say in verses 39-40, "But I tell you, D*o not
resist and evil person. If someone strikes you on the right
cheek, turn to him the other also. And if someone wants
to sue you and take your tunic, let him have your cloak as
well.*" Be willing to overlook offenses. What do you do
when you get hit on the cheek? Human nature is to want
to sock them right back. There are a lot of problems we
face in the world and in the church today that could have
been handled differently. For example, if someone does
something wrong to someone, then that person reacts to
it, and in turn, they get them back. Pretty soon it is a
snowball effect. "They did something wrong to me, now
I will get them back. Now they think they have to get

me back for me getting them back." It is a meaningless endless cycle of people trying to get even with each other. What started out as a small disagreement has escalated into an all out war. We need to stop the spiral of hate before it gets out of control. Jesus says if they hit you on the check—turn the other one towards them. They may hit you again, but you are showing them you are not going to retaliate. If they want to fight, they are going to be the only ones fighting.

Jesus says if they take your tunic—which is your undergarments, give them your cloak as well—or outer garments. Let yourself be stripped naked rather than get involved in a fight. God will make sure you are taken care of and you have what you need. Jesus also says if someone

> *It is a meaningless endless cycle of people trying to get even with each other. What started out as a small disagreement has escalated into an all out war.*

forces you to go one mile, go with him two miles. The Roman soldiers forced civilians to help them carry their gear one mile. By Roman law, the soldier could not make a single person carry their equipment farther than a mile. Jesus says to go beyond what they force you to do; go two miles. The Jews wouldn't have liked that. "Why Jesus? Why help out the pagan Romans? They are our enemies." Jesus asks us to go the extra mile. To show the loving spirit of Jesus, and to help people even when they are mean to you.

Jesus is not asking us to do something that He was not willing to do Himself. He was a model for us. Jesus did the ultimate turning of the cheek. People beat Him, insulted Him, and killed Him—and yet He had forgiveness for them. He took it. You'd better believe that He had the power to do to them, what they were doing to him. But He took it.

The Apostle Paul says in Romans 12:17, *"Do not repay anyone evil for evil..."* We are not to keep a score sheet to see who has done something bad to us and how many times they have been mean to us. Getting back at somebody does not show the character of Jesus. Do not trade blow for blow, insult for insult, or injury for injury. A mark of every Christian should be a loving and gracious spirit no matter what people do to you.

Let me share with you a true example of someone loving their enemy. The first Anabaptist believers were persecuted badly—burned at the stake, drowned, and had their tongues cut out. If they were caught, they would face death. There was an Anabaptist believer named Dirck Willems who was running for his life; they were coming to arrest him. He ran over a frozen lake—but when his pursuer ran over the same lake, he broke through the ice. Willems, instead of running for his freedom, stopped to save his persecutor. He was then captured, imprisoned and burned at the stake.[41] Talk about love for your enemy. Knowing he would die, he stopped to save the life of the person who would kill him. Dirck Willems was not just nice to his Anabaptist buddies—he was nice to even those who wanted him dead. How many of us, if we were in that position would run back and save the person who wanted to kill us? Why did Dirck Willems do that? Why would we ever do something like that? We would do it to reflect the character of Jesus. We would do it to help others even though they want to harm us. Even though people make fun of us or yell at us, we should give them compliments. They will probably get mad at you for complimenting them because it makes them look bad, but that is what we are supposed to do. Repay the evil with good.

I once saw someone wearing a T-shirt that said something like this, "Christians are like the moon, we reflect the light of the SON." We reflect Jesus. We are to love all people—no matter what they have done to us or no matter what they want to do to us

> *Jesus is not asking us to do anything that He was not willing to do Himself. He was a model for us. Jesus did the ultimate turning of the cheek.*

in the future. Don't stoop to their level. If someone says something bad about you—don't worry about your reputation. It is when you fight back that people question your reputation. Stay positive with all people—don't be negative. Don't let bitterness and negativity get the best of you.

Jesus paid the ultimate price for our forgiveness—He died on the cross. Your God died on the cross so you would be forgiven...and you can't overlook what your brother has done? You can't overlook what your sister has said? Jesus basically says, "You have nothing even close to forgive compared to what I have forgiven you for. If you withhold your forgiveness, I will withhold mine." His death on the cross is an example for us. Forgive, Forgive, Forgive! Dr. Martin Luther King, Jr. said, "Forgiveness is not just an occasional act; it is a permanent attitude."[42] Our entire life is about forgiveness, because our entire life depends on His forgiveness.

chapter 10

Sexual Purity

We live in a difficult age. As each year passes on, there are more and more sexual images that bombard the television and computer screens, billboards, and magazines. We live in a world where sex is the way to advertise and get your point across. The television programs that get the highest ratings are the ones that glorify sexual freedom. We have come a long way from yesterday's "Leave it to Beaver" to today's "Sex in the City." Our culture has defined any kind of sex as good because we were made as sexual beings. Perhaps we should consult the One who made us; maybe He has a few ideas on this topic. Maybe He had an original plan for us in this area.

The Bible's standard on Sex

God makes it clear that sex is only supposed to happen within the covenant of marriage. Hebrews 13:4, *"Marriage should be honored by all, and the marriage bed kept pure, for God will judge the adulterer and all the sexually immoral."* The marriage bed is to be kept pure! That is not a popular concept in today's society. Sexual purity is not something people strive for. A story that I came across as I was researching this chapter is an example of mankind's sexual depravity.

Natalie, a 22-year-old woman from San Diego, California, has decided to pay for her Master's Degree by selling something that is precious and belongs only to her: her virginity. She got the idea from her sister, who was able to save up enough money for her own degree by working as a prostitute for three weeks. Natalie realizes that the idea may seem appalling to some, but she is unconcerned: "I know that a lot of people will condemn me for this because it's so taboo, but I really don't have a problem with that." Sadly, the degree Natalie would like to earn with the money is in Marriage and Family Counseling. Even more sadly, her offer has been met with wide appeal by a variety of men. In fact, over 10,000 men responded to the auction, with the highest bidder offering more than 3.7 million dollars. That kind of massive response was a surprise even to Natalie. She said, "It's shocking that men will pay so much for someone's virginity, which isn't even prized so highly anymore."[43]

Obviously there is not a real desire to keep the marriage bed pure. People do not hold the marriage bed sacred as the Bible tells us too. People say, "Sex makes me feel good. Sex helps me achieve my goals. Sex will keep me in the relationship that I want to be in—if I don't have sex, the person may leave me." We pursue sex, and turn our backs on the life God wants us to live.

God makes it clear in His Word that sex is supposed to be only within the marriage relationship. But there are many people who like to blur the lines on what marriage is according to the Bible. In our society, there are many different ideas of what marriage looks like. Can we have multiple wives at the same time? Can we be married more than once? Can marriage be between two people of the same sex? Jesus answers those questions in Matthew 19:4-6. *"'Haven't you read,' he replied, 'that at the beginning the Creator 'made them male and female,' and said, 'For this reason a man will leave his father and mother and be united to his wife, and the two will become one flesh'? So they are no longer two, but one. Therefore what God has joined together, let man not separate.'"* A man, singular, will leave his father and mother and be united to his wife, singular. The marriage relationship is between one male and one female. A man cannot have many wives, and a man cannot have another man as his spouse. Jesus also says, *"...and the two will become one flesh? So they are no longer two, but one."* There is a Holy mystical bond that happens as we take our vows to one another before God. Somehow in the sight of God we become one flesh. We cannot become two again. For a culture that likes to follow their own logic and feelings; Jesus makes it very clear in His Word that marriage is between one man and one woman for life.

> *For a culture that likes to follow their own logic and feelings; Jesus makes it very clear in His Word that marriage is between one man and one woman for life.*

Divorce is running out of control in our society, and I wish it was only in our society. Statistics show that divorce occurs just as much in the church as it does in the world. We are supposed to be different, set apart from the world as obedient followers of Christ's Word. We are to be a witness to the world that marriage is a covenant before God and to our marriage partner for life. If we as Christians don't believe in it, why should the world? The devil comes in and deceives us saying that there is no love in your marriage anymore. We start to believe what he says and we convince ourselves that it is the truth. "I don't love my spouse anymore." Love is not a feeling. Our feelings are part of the fall of mankind and your feelings will play tricks on you. Love is an action. Jesus didn't feel like going to the cross, but he went because of His great love for you. You may not feel like you love your spouse, because you are not fostering that relationship. You are falling in love with someone else because you are spending more time with them and you are thinking of them constantly. If you put your heart and soul back into your relationship with your spouse, you will soon start feeling love for him/her again. Your heart belongs to your spouse, and no other. You are one flesh with them. You can't become two again.

There are many people who are in the covenant relationship of marriage, yet they cheat on their spouse and find sexual fulfillment somewhere else, whether it is through pornography or whether it is with another person. In Proverbs 5, Solomon shares this with us.

[15] *Drink water from your own cistern,*
running water from your own well.
[16] *Should your springs overflow in the*
streets, your streams of water in the

public squares?

[17] *Let them be yours alone, never to be shared with strangers.*

[18] *May your fountain be blessed, and may you rejoice in the wife of your youth.*

[19] *A loving doe, a graceful deer— may her breasts satisfy you always, may you ever be captivated by her love.*

[20] *Why be captivated, my son, by an adulteress?*
Why embrace the bosom of another man's wife?

[21] *For a man's ways are in full view of the LORD, and he examines all his paths.*

[22] *The evil deeds of a wicked man ensnare him; the cords of his sin hold him fast.*

[23] *He will die for lack of discipline, led astray by his own great folly.*

Solomon was, according to scripture, the wisest man who ever lived, but women were his downfall. It was his relationships with women that made him stray from the Lord.[45] He penned these words even though he had 700 wives and 300 concubines. He was looking for satisfaction where he could not find it. None of the 1,000 women he had could bring the satisfaction that only God can bring. Solomon says, *"Rejoice in the wife of your youth."* You don't need someone else to make you happy. You are to stay true to the one that God gave you in the covenant of marriage, because when you make the covenant with your spouse, God is also the third party in that covenant. You are making that covenant promise to God, as well.

The Apostle Paul was sickened by the sexual

immorality he saw in the first century. He said in 1 Thessalonians 4:3-5, *"It is God's will that you should be sanctified: that you should avoid sexual immorality; that each of you should learn to control his own body in a way that is holy and honorable, not in passionate lust like the heathen, who do not know God."* There should be a difference in behavior between those who know God's Holy Standards and those who live this life for their own desires. Our purity and self control should be evident to all who look at our life.

Single people have questions on "where should I draw the line sexually in a relationship? I know sex outside of marriage is wrong, but what about heavy petting or oral sex. Is that wrong?"

> *There should be a difference in behavior between those who know God's Holy standards and those who live this life for their own desires. Our purity and self control should be evident to all who look at our life.*

I think Paul gives us a clear answer in Ephesians 5:3. *"But among you there must not be even a hint of sexual immorality, or of any kind of impurity, or of greed, because these are improper for God's holy people."* There should not be even a hint of sexual immorality among God's people. We are called to be Holy, the pure spotless bride of Christ. Imagine with me if you would, it is your wedding day. As the groom comes in to look at his bride, he sees that she is cheating on him with another man. Would that upset you as the groom? I am sure it would be devastating. Again let's see Jesus as the Bridegroom coming to get His bride. How would you like it if Jesus came back as you were having oral sex with someone who wasn't your spouse? Would you be ashamed if Jesus came back and you were surfing the web for pornography?

The Bible calls us to live pure and holy lives before God. Job 31:1 says, *"I made a covenant with my eyes not to look lustfully at a girl."* Make an agreement with yourself that you are not even going to look at things that will be a temptation to you. We need to focus on the things that will please God and not on the forbidden fruit, so that when our wedding day comes, as Jesus breaks through the sky to bring His bride home, we will be that pure spotless bride.

God gave them over to their sin.

This is some pretty scary stuff. Even though God set up this standard of pure and holy living, people gave in to their sexual appetites. Listen to Romans 1:21, *"For although they knew God, they neither glorified him as God nor gave thanks to him, but their thinking became futile and their foolish hearts were darkened."* Did you hear that first phrase? These are people who <u>knew</u> God! These people knew God, but they didn't live like it. They did not live their lives by the standards He had set. They knew God existed, but did not make him Lord of their lives. This phrase, "God gave them over" comes up three times in Romans chapter one. It happens in verse 24, verse 26, and verse 28. "God gave them over" basically means, "God gives them that terrible freedom they have longed for." If you want to get wrapped up in your sinful ways—God will allow you too. And once you get started down the pathway of sin—sin will hold you in its grips and will not let you go. God releases them to their depraved ways of thinking and living.

Verse 24 says, *"Therefore God gave them over in*

the sinful desires of their hearts to sexual impurity for the degrading of their bodies with one another." You look at our society today and you see there is no self control when it comes to controlling sexual desires. There are people having sex before they are married, and then once they are married they go and have sex with people who are not their spouse. They seek the sex that is not in line with the will of God. They always want that forbidden fruit.

In today's society, another big thing is pornography. The devil wants you to lust. He knows lusting is a sin. As Christians, we need to grab a hold of the truth found in 1 Corinthians 3:16, which says, *"Don't you know that you yourselves are God's temple and that God's Spirit lives in you?"* Our bodies are the temple of God—because God's Spirit lives in us. How can we take God's temple and use it for perversion. We are to use it in a holy way.

> **They seek the sex that is not in line with the will of God. They always want that forbidden fruit.**

But things get even worse as we read further in Romans 1. In verses 26-27, it says, *"Because of this, God gave them over to <u>shameful lusts</u>. Even their women exchanged natural relations for unnatural ones. In the same way the men also abandoned natural relations with women and were inflamed with lust for one another…"* Sexual immorality is not alright with God, and we can see here that God is also clearly against homosexuality. This has become a big issue in our world today. Our culture and our government are starting to accept homosexuality as an acceptable life style. There are many states that are adopting "same sex marriages". This tolerance is making its way into churches as well.

A big argument I often hear about homosexuality is that, "we are born this way, and we are bent to do these things at birth. God will not judge us because that is the way He made us." We cannot use that excuse to gratify our own desires <u>because all of us are born with a bend to sin</u>. Every one of us, because of Adam and Eve, has been born with a sinful nature. Psalm 51:5 says, *"Surely I was sinful at birth, sinful from the time my mother conceived me."* I don't care who you are, we all have a sinful nature in us that urges us to do the things that are contrary to God. But once we come to Christ, we desire to live by God's ways even when it is a denial of our ways. Luke 9:23 says, *"Then he* (Jesus) *said to them all: 'if anyone would come after me, he must deny himself and take up his cross daily and follow me.'"* We need to deny ourselves the things in our lives that are not in line with the Word of God. As I said in chapter 6, a disciple needs to do more than gain knowledge from his teacher; his life should look like his teacher's. If I could actually picture Jesus teaching two guys that it's alright to get married, and seeing him do that Himself—I would say that it is alright. But Jesus made it clear in the gospels that marriage is between one man and one woman for life. If we accept homosexuality, even though the Bible says differently, then that opens the floodgates of immorality for other things as well; sex before marriage has to be alright and cheating on one's spouse would have to be permissible as well. Obviously that is

> *Scripture is clear about sexual immorality. Culture tries to muddy the water with sexual immorality, but God's Word makes it crystal clear.*

not the case. Scripture is clear about sexual immorality. Culture tries to muddy the water with sexual immorality, but God's Word makes it crystal clear.

Some people object to this teaching, because we are to show love to all people and accept them. However, in teaching them what the scriptures say about homosexuality, we are showing them love. We are warning them that they are not living according to God's plan. 1 Corinthians 6:9-10, *"Do you not know that the wicked will not inherit the kingdom of God? Do not be deceived: Neither the sexually immoral nor idolaters nor adulterers nor male prostitutes nor homosexual offenders nor thieves nor the greedy nor drunkards nor slanderers nor swindlers will inherit the kingdom of God."* As a church, we do not look favorably on sexual immorality of any kind; whether that is homosexuality, sex before marriage, adultery, or pornography. If you have any un-repentant sin in your life, you need to get serious before God right now.

Maybe you have done things sexually in your past that you are not proud of. The great news is that homosexuality, or adultery, or any other sexual sin is not considered "the unforgiveable sin". It is a sin, and Jesus came to set us free from sin. However, forgiveness comes by repenting of what

> **The great news is that homosexuality, or adultery, or any other sexual sin is not considered "the unforgiveable sin". It is a sin, and Jesus came to set us free from sin.**

you are doing and leaving that lifestyle. Love is to warn people they are on the wrong road. We are not to hold people's hands as they go to hell and tell them that they are alright. If a child was out playing in the street, would telling them to stop actually be restricting them and not showing them love? You better believe out of love I will be dragging that child in off the street.

You cannot take these sexual sins lightly or there will be an underlying assumption that these sins are really not that bad. Paul repeatedly points out the seriousness of sexually immoral sin, because if he doesn't, more people will join in that behavior. It wouldn't take long for it to be an <u>acceptable</u> practice. Paul gives us a stern warning in 1 Corinthians 6:18. *"Flee from sexual immorality. All other sins a man commits are outside his body, but he who sins sexually sins against his own body."*

Remember your body is the temple of the Holy Spirit. You don't want to sin against the place where the Holy Spirit resides. Your sexual purity is very important to God. Let your body be the pure temple of God. Let your body be the pure spotless bride that Jesus is coming for.

chapter 11

Controling The Tongue

Talking is something we do every day, and we don't give much thought about the impact that we can have on others. Our words have great potential. They can build someone up or they can tear someone down. Are you aware of how your words affect other people? Many of you may be thinking, "I know someone who needs to read this chapter." But this chapter is for you, as well. We all need to carefully watch the words we speak. James has a lot to say about the importance of the words that we speak. James 3 says,

> *[1] Not many of you should presume to be teachers, my brothers, because you know that we who teach will be judged more strictly. [2] We all stumble in many ways. If anyone is never at fault in what he says, he is a perfect man, able to keep his whole body in check.*
>
> *[3] When we put bits into the mouths of horses to make them obey us, we can turn the whole animal. [4] Or take ships as an example. Although they are so large and are driven by strong winds, they are steered by a very small rudder wherever the pilot*

wants to go. [5] Likewise the tongue is a small part of the body, but it makes great boasts. Consider what a great forest is set on fire by a small spark. [6] The tongue also is a fire, a world of evil among the parts of the body. It corrupts the whole person, sets the whole course of his life on fire, and is itself set on fire by hell.

[7] All kinds of animals, birds, reptiles and creatures of the sea are being tamed and have been tamed by man, [8] but no man can tame the tongue. It is a restless evil, full of deadly poison. [9] With the tongue we praise our Lord and Father, and with it we curse men, who have been made in God's likeness. [10] Out of the same mouth come praise and cursing. My brothers, this should not be. [11] Can both fresh water and salt water flow from the same spring? [12] My brothers, can a fig tree bear olives, or a grapevine bear figs? Neither can a salt spring produce fresh water.

The tongue is small but it has great influence.

A squirrel is a very small animal. Could a small little squirrel have any impact on thousands of people? On September 11, 1995, a squirrel climbed on the Metro-North Railroad power lines near New York City. This set off an electrical surge, which weakened an overhead bracket, which let a wire dangle down toward the tracks.

A train came by and the wire got caught on it, which tore down all the lines. As a result, 47,000 commuters were stuck in Manhattan for many hours that evening. A small little squirrel had an impact on 47,000 people that day.[46]

The tongue is even smaller than the squirrel, and it has even a greater impact on people. The right words can brighten up someone's entire day and the wrong words can ruin someone's day. Our words can soar people to new heights or they can put someone on a downward spiral in life. Our words are very powerful. James uses three examples of how something so small has such a huge impact: the bit in the mouth of a horse, the rudder that can turn a ship, and a spark that can start a forest fire. I don't know much about horses, but I find it amazing that one little bit in a horse's mouth will turn a 1,000 pound horse any direction you want it to go. James says that the bit turns the <u>whole animal</u>. It doesn't just turn the horse's head. That tiny bit has the power to completely change the direction of a huge horse, and our words have the power to alter the direction of people's lives (for the good or bad).

There was a little boy named Elijah E. Cummins who was in special education. A school counselor told him there was

> *Our words can soar people to new heights or they can put someone on a downward spiral in life.*

no way he could ever grow up to be anything special. He started to believe it, but he had a great teacher, as well as positive parents who encouraged him and said, "You can be anything you want to be." Elijah became a House Representative in the United States Congress from the state of Maryland.[47] He could have missed out on his potential if he would have listened to his school counselor. We need to surround ourselves with people who will build us up, rather than tear us down. If you are told too many times you can't do it, you will probably start believing it. However, if you have people around you who continually build you up and tell you that you can do it, you will start believing that you can.

The illustration that hits home with me the most is the illustration of a fire. It only takes one little spark to start a forest fire. Think about the forest fires that California has had. Over the past few years, tens of thousands of acres have been burned up every year because of one spark that started and got out of control. I wonder how many raging forest fires we have started in our lives by a few words that we have spoken. We may just say a couple wrong things, but they can have devastating effects. I remember a children's story that was told at our church. The leader brought a small tube of toothpaste for each child and she told them to get the tooth paste out of the tube as fast as they could. The kids got it out very quickly. Then she told them, "Here is a spoon, now put the toothpaste back in the tube." They could not get the toothpaste back in the tube no matter how hard they tried. The point of that was to show the kids that it is easy to say something, but very hard to take it back. That illustration made a huge impact on me! I hope it made an impact on the children as well.

You don't think your words are very important. Look at James 3:6 again, *"The tongue also is a fire, a world of evil among the parts of the body. It corrupts the whole person, sets the whole course of his life on fire, and is itself set on fire by hell."* The tongue is a fire. Have you ever seen a forest fire? It consumes everything in its path. Your tongue is just like a fire that consumes everything in its path. Verse 6 also says that the tongue corrupts the whole person. Maybe you have said, "I know I need to work on how I talk, but everything else is ok. I'm not that bad." James says your words corrupt your whole life. Your tongue has great power, and it steers your life. Which way is it steering you? The tongue bares influence far more than the proportion of its size. We've all heard the saying, "sticks and stones may break my bones, but words can never hurt me." Not true. Words will not break your bones, but they do hurt. Words ruin reputations, crush self esteem, and destroy friendships. Entire lives are ruined by careless words spoken.

Consistency in our speech.
Listen to verses 9-10, *"With the tongue we praise our Lord and Father, and with it we curse men, who have been made in God's likeness. Out of the same mouth come praise and cursing. My brothers, this should not be."* We come to church praising God, singing at the top of our lungs, and then we go out into the church parking lot and talk about what so and so did at church today. You go through the week gossiping, telling lies, yelling at people, but Sunday comes around again and your tongue praises the Lord. There needs to be consistency. I heard someone curse one time—

> *You go through the week gossiping, telling lies, yelling at people, but Sunday comes around again and your tongue praises the Lord.*

and someone else said to them, "Do you kiss your mom with that mouth." (With that dirty mouth). The same principle applies here; we speak badly and we use the same tongue to praise God.

Our tongues are made to speak edifying things. Ephesians 4:29 says, *"Do not let any unwholesome talk come out of your mouths, but only what is helpful for building others up according to their needs, that it may benefit those who listen."* We can't praise God with our tongues and then turn around and use it to hurt one of His creations. Do not let any unwholesome thing come out of our mouths. People in the world use their tongues to tear each other down, but the church is supposed to be different. We are supposed to show love to each other. We are supposed to use our speech to build each other up. Here is some great advice we should all follow, "If you don't have anything nice to say, don't say anything at all."

There is a story of some monks in a remote monastery deep in the woods who follow a rigid vow of silence. Their vow could only be broken once a year— on Christmas—by one monk. That monk could speak only one sentence. One Christmas, Brother Thomas had his turn to speak and said, "I love the delightful mashed potatoes we have every year with the Christmas roast!" Then he sat down. Silence ensued for 365 days. The next Christmas, Brother Michael got his turn and said, "I think the mashed potatoes are lumpy, and I truly despise them!" Once again, silence ensued for 365 days. The following Christmas, Brother Paul rose and said, "I am fed up with this constant bickering!"[48]

We need to make the words we speak count. In this past week, if we took out all of the cursing, lying, gossiping, yelling, and sarcasm in our speech, what would be left? It is so easy to get caught up in the moment. If someone starts to gossip, we can't help but jump in. It is like our tongues have a mind of their own. James says in verses 7-8, *"All kinds of animals, birds, reptiles and creatures of the sea are being tamed and have been tamed by man, but no man can tame the tongue. It is a restless evil, full of deadly poison."* Taming the tongue is not easy. James says it is easier to tame wild animals. It is easier for me to train a grizzly bear to do what I want, than it is to train my tongue to do what I want. Our tongues are in a slippery spot, but we need to learn to control them.

We will never completely be faultless in what we say, but there is always room for improvement. Don't pass on the rumors that you hear. If someone says, "let me tell you about so and so." Ask them if you can repeat what they are saying to the person they are talking about. If not, don't be just another link in the gossip chain. Jesus says in Matthew 12:36, *"But I tell you that men will have to give account on the day of judgment for every careless word they have spoken."* Some people talk like they are not accountable for the words that they speak. One day, we will be sorry for not taking control of our speech.

Our tongues have huge potential. They can be full of deadly poison, or they can be full of grace. We need to let Jesus be the Lord of our speech. Our words

People in the world use their tongues to tear each other down, the church is supposed to be different.

flow out of our relationship with Christ. Good words are spoken because they stem from the Spirit who has taken over your life, and when you spend significant time studying God's Word. Bad words flow from the sinful nature that still has control of our lives. Jesus said in Matthew 15:11, *"What goes into a man's mouth does not make him 'unclean,' but what comes out of his mouth, that is what makes him 'unclean.'"* What comes out of your mouth? Remember, the words that you speak show the condition of your heart.

chapter 12

Don't Run This Race Alone

We are used to the races today where there is only one winner. You are competing against everyone else to be the one to bring home the trophy or gold metal. But the Christian race is not a competition against each other. We are all on the same team. We all are striving for eternal life in Jesus Christ, and each one of us can receive the great reward that is waiting for us. We don't need to knock each other down to win the prize for ourselves, but we need to run together, so that we all can cross the finish line together as winners. In Mark chapter 2, we see people working together for the physical healing of their friend, and it results in a greater spiritual healing for him.

> *¹A few days later, when Jesus again entered Capernaum, the people heard that he had come home. ² So many gathered that there was no room left, not even outside the door, and he preached the word to them. ³ Some men came, bringing to him a paralytic, carried by four of them. ⁴ Since they could not get him to Jesus because of the crowd, they made an opening in the roof above Jesus and, after digging through it, lowered the*

mat the paralyzed man was lying on.
⁵ When Jesus saw their faith, he said to the paralytic, "Son, your sins are forgiven."

⁶ Now some teachers of the law were sitting there, thinking to themselves, ⁷ "Why does this fellow talk like that? He's blaspheming! Who can forgive sins but God alone?"

⁸ Immediately Jesus knew in his spirit that this was what they were thinking in their hearts, and he said to them, "Why are you thinking these things? ⁹ Which is easier: to say to the paralytic, 'Your sins are forgiven,' or to say, 'Get up, take your mat and walk'? ¹⁰ But that you may know that the Son of Man has authority on earth to forgive sins...." He said to the paralytic, ¹¹ "I tell you, get up, take your mat and go home."
¹² He got up, took his mat and walked out in full view of them all. This amazed everyone and they praised God, saying, "We have never seen anything like this!"

This man had some incredible friends. Can you see how lucky he was to have friends like that? Picture this scene with me. The word is out that Jesus is coming to Capernaum. The paralytic heard the news, but how was he going to get to Jesus? He couldn't even get across the room. It didn't matter that Jesus was right down the street from him—Jesus might as well have been 500 miles away. He couldn't get to Jesus on his own. Luckily this man had friends that were really concerned about his well being. So they picked him up and started to walk toward the house where Jesus was teaching.

As they approached the house, the situation had to be disheartening. The crowd was packed into the house and lined up all of the way outside the house. Everyone in this crowd wanted to see Jesus—they all wanted to be closer to Him. The friends of the paralytic knew that they would not be able to squeeze through the crowd, because I am sure there were other sick people in the crowd that day who wanted to be healed. It looked impossible for these four friends to carry a man all the way through the house. Can you picture this huge crowd? Let me give you an illustration of what it might have looked like. Get 200 kids together and dump a bag of candy out on the floor—let's see how easy it is for you to get through this crowd of kids. These kids will be pushing their own way to the front to get some candy. They almost certainly wouldn't let another person by who wants the same candy as they do. In the same way, everyone in this crowd wanted to be closer to Jesus, and to hear His words, and to be touched by Him. So these friends were faced with an impossible task of getting their friend to Jesus. So what did they do? They found a way. They didn't let a little obstacle stop them. They were determined to get their friend to Jesus. They got him up to the roof, dug a hole in the roof and handed him down before Jesus. This was not a simple task for them, but through their hard work and their deep concern for their friend, he was finally in the midst of Jesus.

Don't you wish that you had friends like that? To have friends that will be there to help you overcome the tough problems that you face in life? The church of God is full of people like this. I enjoy seeing God's people living out their

It didn't matter that Jesus was right down the street from him—Jesus might as well have been 500 miles away. He couldn't get to Jesus on his own.

faith like these four men did for their friend. I see this kind of faith all of the time in the church that I pastor. If someone has surgery or is bed-ridden for a month, my church has a sign-up sheet to take meals over to their house for as long as the meals are needed. Not too long ago, there was a widow in our church who had a leaky roof. We had some people in the church inspect her roof and they found that the entire roof needed to be repaired. For the next several weeks, people from the church tore off the old roof, made some repairs, and put a new roof on the house. That is an example of the family of God looking out for each other. Sometimes, we are the ones on the roof pounding the nails for someone else or cooking the meals and running it over to their house. While at another point in life, people may be working on our house or cooking meals for our family. We need each other. At the end of Acts 2, we see that the early church was committed to each other. If someone needed help, they would sell their possessions to help the person who was in need. They cared more about other people than they did themselves.

We need each other

The Christian walk is a journey that we are all on together. We need to be concerned for each other just as the four friends were concerned about the paralytic man.

The point that I want to drive home as you are reading this chapter, is that we need each other as we live our lives for Jesus. Hebrews 10:24-25 says, *"And let us consider how we may spur one another on toward love and good deeds. Let us not give up meeting together, as some are in the habit of doing, but let us encourage one another and all the more as you see the Day approaching."* Living our lives for God is contrary to our culture. So if we do not have a support group that we meet with on a regular basis, we will more than likely conform and be like the people whom we hang around with. The people we spend time with the most will be the type of people we will become. We need to be around people who will encourage us and who really want what is best for us.

Unfortunately, there are so many Christians today who think that they can do it all by themselves. They don't believe that they need to go to church. There is a story that I have always enjoyed that shows the importance of attending church.

One day a pastor went to make a visit to someone who did not attend church very faithfully. The man was sitting before a fire, watching the warm glow of the coals. It was a cold winter day, but the coals were red hot, and the fire was warm. The pastor pleaded with the man to be more faithful in meeting with the people of God, but the man didn't seem to get the message. So the pastor took the tongs beside the fire place, pulled open the screen, and reached in and began to separate all the coals. When none of the coals were touching the others, he stood and watched in silence. In a matter of moments, they were all cold...The man got the message.[49]

The coals together kept each other hot, but as soon as the coals were separated, they quickly became cold. What a valuable lesson for us as Christians to see—the importance of sticking together. If we aren't around other Christians, we will not have people in our lives who can lead us back if we go astray. We will not have the people in our lives that will pick us up and carry us to Jesus. We need people who we can turn to when we find that the world is against us.

I am so thankful that I am surrounded by friends who will take me to Jesus when I am hurting and when I finally realize that I can't get there on my own. I remember a number of years ago when I was going through a really difficult period in my

> **We need each other to stay on fire for God. If we go off on our own, our fire will go out.**

life. Nothing made sense to me. It seemed everything that could go wrong, went wrong. I was hurting from a relationship that didn't work out; I was hurting because I didn't know my place in this world; I was just hurting... sometimes I didn't even know what I was hurting from. During this experience I realized the importance of having Christian friends. I had friends that were like this paralytic man's friends. They picked me up and helped me to Jesus. My friends knew how much I was hurting and they would call me and they would check up on me—they would pray for me over the phone. I knew they were praying for me throughout the day. Emotionally, I did not think that I could get to Jesus, but my friends picked me up and took me to Him. I made it through this experience by God's grace and with the love of my friends. I would not have wanted to go through this experience without my Christian friends. I am sure that I would have gotten through it, but I am not sure that I would be in a close relationship with God today if they wouldn't have led me to Him.

The four friends really need to be commended for their commitment to the paralytic man. When Jesus saw their faith, He said to the paralytic in verse 5, *"When Jesus saw their faith, He said to the paralytic, 'Son your sins are forgiven.'"* When Jesus saw their faith…Jesus healed this man because of "their faith". You notice it doesn't say he was healed because of "his faith". He is obviously talking about the friends of the paralytic. But does this phrase "their faith" also include the paralytic? We cannot say for sure. The text does not tell us whether this man has faith or not. If he does have faith, I can see these friends as people that he studies the Bible with. If he doesn't have faith, we can learn a valuable lesson from this—our faith can save our friends. I am not saying that people can live off of our faith and that they do not need a faith of their own. However, I am saying that our faith in action can lead people to Jesus. If we bring our non-Christian friends before Jesus and He touches them, they will be changed. It is interesting to see that most people do not find Jesus on their own—they actually had someone take them to Jesus. As I flipped through the gospels, I counted more people who were healed because they were either brought to Jesus by someone, or someone brought Jesus to them. Less than half of the healings mentioned in the gospels, were people seeking their own healing. Of the vast number of people who find their way to Jesus today, most of them reach Him because their friends are concerned about the welfare of their souls. So no matter if our friends are Christian or non-Christian, we need to bring them before Jesus.

Are we willing to help take each other to Jesus just like these friends did for the paralytic, and as my friends did for me so faithfully? Our relationships to each other are very important for our personal walk with God and for our fellow believers' walk. We can be one of three things in our relationship. 1) We can hinder others, 2) we can show no interest in their lives, 3) or we can help them. We can hinder people—let's say you go hiking at the Grand Canyon with a group of friends. As you are walking, you slip on a stone and you twist your ankle. Obviously it is going to affect you, but it will also affect your friends as well. You are going to slow them down because they have to wait for you since you are not walking very well on your own. In the same way, we can bring people down spiritually. We can be a bad example for people. Instead of leading them to Jesus, our example pushes them further away from God. Or secondly, we may choose not to show an interest in the lives of others. We may be like the people in the story of the Good Samaritan. Two people just walked right on by and did not show concern for their brother who was in desperate need. There are needs all around us in the people we see every day. Are we too busy to stop and help them? Do we have no concern for them? Or thirdly, we can be the people who will bring them before the Lord. We can have our eyes open to the hurts and needs that are around us, and we can be willing to forget about ourselves to invest in someone else. We can be the instrument that God uses to bring a broken sinful person before Jesus so that Jesus can bring the spiritual healing that they so desperately need.

Being a part of a family

When we welcome new people into our church as members, it is an important day in the life of the church. New members are not just adding their names to the membership role—they are becoming a part of our family. We call each other brothers and sisters, because we have the same Father in God. He has adopted all of us into His family. I love family gatherings and I hate to miss any opportunity that my family gets together. The same is true in my spiritual family. Every chance I get, I want to meet with my spiritual family as they gather together. I didn't get to choose my biological family, but I did get to choose which church I call my spiritual family. What a special bond I have formed with the people I labor with in advancing God's Kingdom.

Something that I like to focus on when we welcome new members into our church is the fact that we are now considered brothers and sisters in Christ. I don't know about you, but as I was growing up, I had many disagreements

> *New members are not just adding their names to the membership role—they are becoming a part of our family.*

with my siblings. We didn't always see eye to eye, but if anyone outside of the family threatened me or tried to beat me up...my siblings would always come to my defense. We didn't always agree, but we loved each other through it all and protected each other. It is the same way in our spiritual family, even though we have a common bond in Jesus Christ. Brothers and sisters in the Lord are going to have disagreements as well. We don't always think the same way as other people. The fact is— the church is made up of sinful people! People at church may hurt your feelings, say things that they shouldn't say about you, or not include you in certain events that they should. Unfortunately, there is a chance that that could happen. But above all else, there is a love for each other because we are all part of the same family.

If you are not currently attending a church, please find a Bible believing church to attend. It is there that you can find common fellowship in Jesus Christ. We have nothing more important in common with anyone, than we do with the people of God through Christ Jesus. There is a possibility that you have been hurt by a church and you haven't attended church since then. First, as a pastor, I would like to say that I am sorry for the pain you feel. It never feels good to be hurt by people who you trust, but don't let that keep you out of the place that God has for you. Jesus came to set up His church. He set it up so that we could all be a part of it. It is at church that people are gathered together to praise our Awesome God, and you know that God will show up in a powerful way. It is at church that you will hear God's Word being spoken and understand Him in a better way. Again, I know some people have been hurt by a church, but please don't let that keep you from running the best race that God has for you. I am not asking you to go back to the same church, but find one that is committed to the Word of God. If you eat at a restaurant and you are offended by them, you will still go out to eat—you just may not eat at that particular restaurant anymore. Don't quit going to church just because one church has left a sour taste in your mouth. God is bigger than one particular church.

Please place yourself in a church where God wants to speak to you. If you are hungry, you will find a restaurant to eat at, even though you were offended by another restaurant. If you are hungry for the Word of God, you will find a church that will bring healing to your soul and lead you into a closer relationship with God. There is so much I know now, that I would not have known if I didn't attend church and stay in fellowship with other believers. You are only hurting yourself and your relationship with God by not opening yourself up to a group of believers to grow with them.

> *There is so much I know now, that I would not have known if I didn't attend church and stay in fellowship with other believers.*

At times we do get knocked down, but there are always people there to pick us back up. The following story is a good illustration of the church.

Every year, thousands of young athletes from all over the world gather for the Special Olympics. These athletes know what it means to give their best. They have run many races just to be qualified to race in the Special Olympics. Each of them wanted to win as they were lining up at the starting line. The gun sounded and they were off. Suddenly, one of the runners fell to the ground and he couldn't get up. The crowd

reacted to the child who fell. One of
the runners looked back to see what
happened. He stopped and went back
and helped the other kid up. Then
they crossed the finish line together.[50]

That is a great picture of the church, and it is
something that I want to be a part of. Remember, we are
running this race for God. When we get knocked down
in this race, we desperately need someone there to pick
us back up so that we can cross the finish line.

We shouldn't give up on people or break fellowship
with them when they hurt us. Take Jesus as our example.
He did not give up on people when they hurt Him and
when they did things that they shouldn't have done to
Him. Peter denied knowing Him three times, yet Jesus
graciously extended grace to him. He even used Peter
to build up His most treasured possession on earth, His
church. Jesus could have called down a legion of angels
while He was on the cross. He could have killed the
people who were crucifying Him; but instead He said,
*"Father, forgive them, for they do not know what they
are doing."*[51]

My friends, let Christ work in you so that you
can forgive others the same way that He forgave you.
Forgive your brothers and sisters in Christ. Continue
meeting together as believers because you are striving
for the same prize. Let's cross this finish line together!

PART 3

The Finish Line

I have fought the good fight, I have finished the race, I have kept the faith. Now there is in store for me the crown of righteousness, which the Lord, the righteous Judge, will award to me on that day—and not only to me, but also to all who have longed for his appearing.
— 2 Timothy 4:7-8

chapter 13

Hell

We have looked at the race God has marked out for us. Hopefully we all have decided to run the race God's way. If not, let me make one last appeal why you should run the race according to God's plan. Let's look at the finish line for those who want to run their own race. In Luke 16, Jesus shares this parable about the rich man and Lazarus.

> [19] *"There was a rich man who was dressed in purple and fine linen and lived in luxury every day.* [20] *At his gate was laid a beggar named Lazarus, covered with sores* [21] *and longing to eat what fell from the rich man's table. Even the dogs came and licked his sores.*
>
> [22] *"The time came when the beggar died and the angels carried him to Abraham's side. The rich man also died and was buried.* [23] *In hell, where he was in torment, he looked up and saw Abraham far away, with Lazarus by his side.* [24] *So he called to him, 'Father Abraham, have pity on me and send Lazarus to dip the tip of his finger in water and cool my tongue,*

because I am in agony in this fire.'

²⁵ "But Abraham replied, 'Son, remember that in your lifetime you received your good things, while Lazarus received bad things, but now he is comforted here and you are in agony. ²⁶ And besides all this, between us and you a great chasm has been fixed, so that those who want to go from here to you cannot, nor can anyone cross over from there to us.'

²⁷ "He answered, 'Then I beg you, father, send Lazarus to my father's house, ²⁸ for I have five brothers. Let him warn them, so that they will not also come to this place of torment.'

²⁹ "Abraham replied, 'They have Moses and the Prophets; let them listen to them.'

³⁰ "'No, father Abraham,' he said, 'but if someone from the dead goes to them, they will repent.'

³¹ "He said to him, 'If they do not listen to Moses and the Prophets, they will not be convinced even if someone rises from the dead.'"

Living for the here and now.

Most people do not think about 10 years down the road, let alone what will happen to them after they die. This is the life they know; this is the life they see. Many people tend to think, "I am going to do whatever I want to make me happy right now." What you need to know is that the choices you make today will affect where you will be in 5 to 10 years from now. More importantly, those choices will also affect where you spend eternity.

There are two different men in this passage. One is poor and has nothing and the other has plenty and is living in luxury. The rich man had no concern for the beggar named Lazarus. The rich man got lost in his own little world thinking, "Which of my many outfits am I going to wear today? Which restaurant should I eat at today?" He had no thought of other people who needed clothing to wear or something to eat. He was taken care of, and that was all that mattered! It reminds me of what Jesus says in Matthew 25.

> [41] *"Then he will say to those on his left, 'Depart from me, you who are cursed, into the eternal fire prepared for the devil and his angels. [42] For I was hungry and you gave me nothing to eat, I was thirsty and you gave me nothing to drink, [43] I was a stranger and you did not invite me in, I needed clothes and you did not clothe me, I was sick and in prison and you did not look after me.'*
>
> [44] *"They also will answer, 'Lord, when did we see you hungry or thirsty or a stranger or needing clothes or sick or in prison, and did not help you?'*
>
> [45] *"He will reply, 'I tell you the truth, whatever you did not do for one of the least of these, you did not*

> *do for me.'*
> [46] *"Then they will go away to eternal punishment, but the righteous to eternal life."*

Whatever we don't do to the least of these in this world, it is just like we are not doing it for Jesus. This rich man didn't lift a finger to do anything for the least of these—for Lazarus. How easy it is to get caught up in our own little world.

At the end of this passage, the men switch fates. The poor man is

> **How easy it is to get caught up in our own little world.**

well off in heaven and the rich man is suffering in hell. It says the rich man died. It didn't say he died right away because he didn't care for the beggar. We don't know the time frame, but he did die. That is a fact of life—we all are going to die. It doesn't matter who you are. You could be the healthiest and wealthiest person in the world, but I guarantee you that you will die (unless Jesus comes back first). So let's do something that this rich man didn't do—we need to plan for our next life. If we plan ahead to buy a house and plan ahead for retirement, why shouldn't we plan ahead on where we are going to spend eternity?

It is interesting who Jesus told this story to. He didn't tell it to Jerusalem's corporate millionaires. He told it to the religious leaders of that day. These are the people who taught God's law to the people. These were religious people, just like you and me, yet they loved money and didn't show any genuine concern for the poor. They did not go out of their way at all to help the poor and needy.

The rich man in this passage knew his religion well. It says he knew Father Abraham, and he knew about the law and the prophets. He had a good grasp of religion but missed the heart of God. The question I have as I read this passage is: Could we be the religious person that Jesus was talking to in this passage? Are we showing little concern for a hurting and dying world all around us? 1 John 3:17-18 says, *"If anyone has material possessions and sees his brother in need but has no pity on him, how can the love of God be in him? Dear children, let us not love with words or tongue but with actions and in truth."*

The world is full of hungry people, as well as people who have never heard the gospel. How often do we choose to spend our money in our own little world, instead of using the resources that God has given us to help this hurting and dying world? You might say, "I need this little gadget to make life a little bit easier. I need this item, even though I will probably only use it a couple times in my life." We choose more small conveniences for ourselves, instead of meeting real needs in people's lives. Do we notice the hurting people in the world, or is our only concern on the "here and now" of our lives? God is concerned about people, not things. God is not impressed with your material things. Shouldn't we be more concerned with people as well?

Hell is real.

Many people believe that hell is not a real place. I read somewhere that 7 out of 10 adults do not think that hell is real. I thought to myself, "There is no way that so few people believe in hell." However, the more I thought about it, our churches would have more people in them if more people believed that hell was a real place. Unfortunately, I think there are even "church going people" that believe that hell is some symbolic place. However, if you believe that the Bible is the true and perfect Word of God, it should be clear and beyond a doubt that hell is real. The New Testament refers to hell 162 times. Jesus himself talks about hell 70 of those 162 times. When we die, there are only two places to spend eternity—heaven or hell. There is no third option. There is no middle room available for those not quite good enough to make it into heaven but not bad enough to go to hell. You will not be reincarnated and come back to this earth again. Hebrews 9:27 says, *"Just as man is destined to die once, and after that to face judgment..."* You die once. There is no second time around, and you are judged by the decisions you make.

Hell is a serious place. I hear people joking around about it all of the time. I have had friends say they are going to hell, but they are going to have a lot of company.

> **When we die, there are only two places to spend eternity—heaven or hell. There is no third option.**

It is not like that will be any consolation. They are implying that hell is going to be a party—"all my friends are going to be there." Look carefully at what the Bible says about hell. In verse 24 it says, *"So he called to him, 'Father Abraham, have pity on me and send Lazarus to dip the tip of his finger in water and cool my tongue, because I am in agony in this fire.'"* Some party! The rich man died, he had been buried, and it says he is in hell. He is gone from this life, but he is still very much alive. Hell is not the end where you cease to exist. Actually, it is just the beginning of an endless eternity. The rich man in hell is a conscious man who is very aware of his surroundings and his feelings. He now knows that hell is miserable. What he wouldn't do for just a single drop of water. K.P. Yohanan, who is the president of Gospel for Asia, said in one of his sermons, "Billions & billions of years from now, people will still be crying out for just a drop of water. They will be crying out to die. 'Please let me die.' But the answer will come back over and over again. 'You will not die. You will never die. You are here for all eternity.'"[52] Scary thought!

My wife Janelle once heard on TV the expression "That is as funny as hell". How funny is hell? The Bible gives us a completely different picture. In Mark 9:47-48 Jesus says, *"And if your eye causes you to sin, pluck it out. It is better for you to enter the kingdom of God with one eye than to have two eyes and be thrown into hell, where 'their worm does not die, and the fire is not quenched.'"* This doesn't sound like hell is going to be a party among friends. It says it is better to pluck out one of your eyes than to go to this place. Get sin out of your life at all costs. This passage gives us two visuals. One visual says that hell is a place where the fire is not quenched. The fire will never stop burning in hell. Picture a man on fire for eternity, desiring to die, but he will never die— screaming in pain for all eternity. Another visual says that hell is a place where the worm never dies. I know this is quite gross, but when you see road kill along the side of the road, they usually have maggots in them that are eating their flesh. Hell is a place where maggots will never die. They will eat your flesh, but your flesh will never be consumed. You will be crying out, "Please let me die." But you will hear the answer back, "You will never die." This sounds completely unpleasant.

It doesn't matter if you are rich or poor, short or

tall, male or female, overweight or skinny, popular or unpopular—if you are not right with God, hell is your destiny.

Seal your fate right now.

The rich man in this passage wanted Lazarus to dip his finger in water and cool his tongue. It says he was in <u>agony</u>. "Just have Lazarus do this small thing to help me out." But Lazarus couldn't. It says in verse 26. *"And besides all this, between us and you a great chasm has been fixed, so that those who want to go from here to you cannot, nor can anyone cross over from there to us."* This passage makes it clear that your eternal fate cannot be changed. Once you are in eternity, that is where you will spend <u>all</u> of eternity. A great chasm has been set up, even if you wanted to go to a different place, it is impossible. You can't get promoted from hell up to heaven. You cannot get moved up to heaven with good behavior. When you die, you will stand before God and he will pronounce your destiny, and that will be your eternal home! Make sure you are ready for that. You need to make a choice today where you want to spend eternity, because tomorrow may be too late. You will have to live for eternity with the consequences of what you choose.

> *You can't get promoted from hell up to heaven. You cannot get moved up to heaven with good behavior.*

Many people argue this and say that if God is a God of love, He would never cast me into hell. They say that it would be against His character. "A loving God would never do that." The problem with their logic is that they are only looking at one of the characteristics of God. God is also a "Just God". Evil has to be dealt with.

Sin & injustice cannot go unpunished. A penalty needs to be paid. You are right— a loving God did not force you to go to hell. You put yourself there by the decisions that you made in this life. He is a loving God. He has provided a way for you to escape from hell by sending His Son into the world. Jesus left heaven, this perfect place where he was receiving the praise from the angels…and He came down and he died upon the cruel, cruel cross. He paid the penalty for our sin. He has washed away our sins and paid the penalty for all of us who have given our lives to Christ. However, if you choose to continue to live in your sins and in your rebellion, you will pay the penalty for yourself—eternity in hell. To me, it is a no brainer. Embrace the cross. Repent and change the way you are living your life. Give God complete control of your life and you will spend eternity with him in heaven.

Hell is real and it is a horrible, horrible place. Temporary pleasures here on earth are not worth the eternity I described in this chapter. If you choose to live your life contrary to the Word of God and take your chances with your eternity, that is your choice. But I love you all too much not to warn you. I don't want to see one person go there. Take time today to really examine your life. Am I living the way that I should? Most people live for the here and now like the rich man did, not giving thought to what lies ahead, saying, "Let's eat, drink and be merry." We can get so caught up in this world, so much that we don't even plan for our life after death. I know which life I am more concerned with, and I know without a shadow of a doubt that I am going to heaven when I die. My confidence doesn't come from my goodness or who I am. I am confident because I know the power of the cross—that the blood of Jesus washes away every sin.

Please reference chapter 2 to make sure that you have a relationship with the Heavenly Father today!

chapter 14

Heaven

For his very first sermon in a preaching class, an African student chose a text describing the joys we'll share when we go to our heavenly home. He said, "I've been in the United States for several months now and I've seen the great wealth that is here—the fine homes and cars and clothes. I've listened to many sermons in churches here, too, but I've yet to hear one sermon about heaven. Because everyone has so much in this country, no one preaches about heaven. People here don't seem to need it. In my country, most people have very little, so we preach on heaven all the time. We know how much we need it, and how much we look forward to it."[53]

Is that true? Do we have so much available to us in America that heaven is something we don't long for? The Bible tells us we are aliens or strangers in this world—as foreigners in this world we should long to go home. No matter what you have in your life right now, it will pale in comparison to what you will have in heaven.

In this chapter we will see the prize that the faithful followers of Jesus will get for running God's race. We get a picture of what is to come in Revelation 21.

> *[1]Then I saw a new heaven and a new earth, for the first heaven and the first earth had passed away, and there was no longer any sea. [2]I saw*

~ 153 ~

the Holy City, the new Jerusalem, coming down out of heaven from God, prepared as a bride beautifully dressed for her husband. ³ And I heard a loud voice from the throne saying, "Now the dwelling of God is with men, and he will live with them. They will be his people, and God himself will be with them and be their God. ⁴ He will wipe every tear from their eyes. There will be no more death or mourning or crying or pain, for the old order of things has passed away."

⁵ He who was seated on the throne said, "I am making everything new!" Then he said, "Write this down, for these words are trustworthy and true."

⁶ He said to me: "It is done. I am the Alpha and the Omega, the Beginning and the End. To him who is thirsty I will give to drink without cost from the spring of the water of life. ⁷ He who overcomes will inherit all this, and I will be his God and he will be my son. ⁸ But the cowardly, the unbelieving, the vile, the murderers, the sexually immoral, those who practice magic arts, the idolaters and all liars—their place will be in the fiery lake of burning sulfur. This is the second death."

God is the Omega.

I want to start by zeroing in on the first part of verse 6. (This was spoken by the One seated on the throne). "He said to me: '*It is done. I am the Alpha and the Omega, the Beginning and the End.*'" Let's look close at the names Alpha and Omega.

Alpha is the first letter of the Greek alphabet and Omega is the last letter of the alphabet. God is the beginning and the end, the first and the last. There is none before Him, and there is none after Him. Meditate on this staggering truth: God is the absolute alpha. Before Him there was nothing—there was no "before Him." Just think of it. For millions and billions and trillions of unending years God existed and never had a beginning. He is the beginning. There never was a time when he was not. Psalm 90:2 says, *"Before the mountains were born or you brought forth the earth and the world, from everlasting to everlasting you are God."* He is from everlasting to everlasting. You look this way, God never had a beginning. You look that way, God will never have an end. Since everything comes from God, and nothing will outlast God, God has no one who can compete with Him. That is why He says there are no other gods besides me. God

had the first word in history, and He
will have the last word as well.[54]

We all had our beginning in God. He created
us. He knit us together in our mother's womb. If He
wouldn't have had given us the breath of life, we would
cease to exist. He is the Alpha—the beginning. But the
truth that I want us to focus on this morning is that God
is the Omega. That is the focus in Revelation 21:6. The
statement, *"I am the Alpha and Omega, the Beginning
and the End,"* comes in a passage dealing with the end of
history. So let's look at God as the Omega. God is the
Omega or the end in two different senses. At the end of
verse 6 going into verse 7 it says, *"To him who is thirsty
I will give to drink without cost from the spring of the
water of life. He who overcomes will inherit all this, and
I will be his God and he will be my son."* For the thirsty,
(for those who thirst after God and long for more of
Him), they will partake of the spring of the water of life.
They will never thirst again, because they will be with
God and He will meet all of the needs that they will ever
have. It also says in verse 7 that we will be His children.
This reminds me of the story of the prodigal son. This
son who was finally coming home, had previously sinned
against his father and expected his father to make him a
slave, but instead the father smothered him with hugs
and kisses. He put a robe on his back and a ring on his
finger which signified that he was truly a son. He killed
the fatted calf and prepared the best meal for his son. In
the same way, God will lavish on us, his children, the
great things He has in store for us when we come home
and enter into His heavenly kingdom. I can see Jesus
saying the same thing to us, as He did to the servant in

Matthew 25:21. *"His master replied, 'Well done, good and faithful servant! You have been faithful with a few things; I will put you in charge of many things. Come and share your master's happiness!'"* What a great day that will be—when we are done with our labors on this earth and we are welcomed into His heavenly kingdom, and share in His happiness.

But there is another group of people mentioned in verse 8. *"But the cowardly, the unbelieving, the vile, the murderers, the sexually immoral, those who practice magic arts, the idolaters and all*

Since everything comes from God, and nothing will outlast God, God has no one who can compete with Him.

liars—their place will be the fiery lake of burning sulfur. This is the second death." These people who were not thirsty, who did not thirst after God, they will also see God as the Omega, but not in the same way. God is their end in the sense that they will finally meet God as their judge. But instead of waters of eternal life, they will inherit a lake that burns with fire. At the end of every road there is God. No matter who you are, you will see God when you die. We may think we are invincible right now—but we are not promised another day or even another breath. 1 Peter 1:24 says, *"For, 'All men are like grass, and all their glory is like the flowers of the field; the grass withers and the flowers fall.'"* We are like the grass of the field—we whither. You will not live forever, so get ready to meet God. "God is the never-ending Omega for every man: either as a fountain of eternal life or a lake of burning sulfur."[55]

Heaven is a perfect place.

In Revelation chapters 21 and 22 we get a picture of how perfect heaven will be. I encourage all of you to read these two chapters. In verse 4 of chapter 21, it says, *"He will wipe every tear from their eyes. There will be no more death or mourning or crying or pain, for the old order of things has passed away."* I am so looking forward to heaven! There will be no more crying; not even a reason to cry. No one is going to hurt you, no one is going to say bad things about you, no one will get in your face to yell at you, no one will gossip behind your back, no one will break your heart in heaven, and no one will let you down. There is no need for tears or sadness.

It also says that "You will not feel any more pain." Glory, Hallelujah to that! Think about that: no more headaches, toothaches, and you won't get the flu. You won't suffer from cancer, arthritis, or depression. Some of us live with chronic health problems. Every day you know that you are going to be hurting. Medication just numbs the pain. Others of us know that that pain could come back at any point. Maybe you have had cancer that has gone into remission, but there is still a persistent thought in your head that it could return. But in heaven you will know for certain that you will always be healthy. You will not need any medication in heaven. There are no pharmacies or hospitals in heaven. Pain and death no longer has power over us. We will be made whole physically, emotionally, and spiritually. Verse 4 says, *"The old order of things has passed away."* All the hurt and junk of this world that caused us pain will be gone. In verse 5, the One seated on the throne said, *"I am making everything new!"* He is restoring everything back to its new position. We will go back to the perfect dwelling place that mankind had before sin entered the world. Verse 3 says, *"Now the dwelling of God is with men, and he will live with them. They will be his people, and God himself will be with them and be their God."* God once dwelled with man until sin entered the world. God walked with Adam and Eve and they had unbroken fellowship with Him. But when sin entered the world, God could not dwell with them any longer. God is holy and cannot have sin in His presence. Now we get a picture of heaven—sin no longer remains and we will have unbroken fellowship with God again. I am really looking forward to heaven because I will not be a sinner anymore. I can't wait to shed my sin, my weak body… and be in His glory and have a new resurrected body!

If we would keep reading in Revelation 21 and 22, we would get even more descriptions about heaven. It talks about how the streets are made of the purest gold.

> *I am so looking forward to heaven because I will not be a sinner anymore. I can't wait to shed my sin, my weak body…and be in His glory and have a new resurrected body!*

It describes a river that flows from the throne of God that is as clear as crystal, and walls that are made out of precious stones. Heaven is going to be an amazing place. Can you imagine streets made of pure gold? I heard a joke one time about a man who really loved his money. He made his wife promise to bury all of his gold with him when he died. So after his death she buried him with his gold. And as the man met St. Peter at the gates of heaven, St. Peter asked the man what he had in his bag. The man said, "This is something that I wanted to bring to heaven with me." St. Peter opened up the bag and saw the gold and said, "Why did you want to bring pavement into heaven with you?"[56]

In heaven, we will walk on streets of gold. What we treasure here on earth will be pavement in heaven. People cheat, steal, and are consumed with getting more things that have absolutely no value at all in eternity. The last chapter was about hell—what a vast contrast to heaven. Hell is where the fire does not go out and where the worm never dies. In heaven there are the streets of gold, a crystal sea, and we will have no more death, crying or pain. That comparison should cause us to live our lives in the light of eternity, not for ourselves in the here and now.

Heaven costs us nothing.

To go to a place like this, it seems like it would cost us a fortune, and that normally would be the case. However, nobody has enough money to get there, no matter how rich they are. But the good news is that heaven is open for all—rich and poor. There is no cost. Verse 6 says, *"He said to me: 'It is done. I am the Alpha and the Omega, the Beginning and the End. To him who is thirsty I will give to drink without cost from the spring of the water of life.'"* The one from the throne says it is done. It reminds me of what Jesus said on the cross. "It is finished."[57]

The cost has been taken care of. He accomplished what needed to be done for us to gain salvation. Many people try to earn something that they cannot possibly earn. It is something freely given to us. Ephesians 2:8-9 says, *"For it is by grace you have been saved, through faith— and this not from yourselves, it is the gift of God—not by works, so that no one can boast."* This living water is given to us without cost because of the grace we find in Jesus Christ. We can all afford heaven, because it is more about surrendering to a new way of life, than about being rich financially.

We must see that we all deserve to be thrown into the fiery lake of burning sulfur. That is what we deserve. Some people think that heaven is an automatic thing that we all get when we die. But look at

> **We all can afford heaven, because it is more about surrendering to a new way of life, not about being rich financially.**

Revelation 21:27. It says, *"Nothing impure will ever enter it, nor will anyone who does what is shameful or deceitful, but only those whose names are written in the Lamb's book of life."* Nothing impure can enter heaven, we must be cleansed. The only way that we can be cleansed of sin is by the blood of Jesus. The only way to heaven is for your name to be written in the Lamb's book of life. If your name is not in the book, no amount of arguing will get your name added. You must surrender your life to Jesus and live for him. Repent of your sins and make him Lord of your life. And if you do that, 1 John 1:9 says, *"If we confess our sins, he is faithful and just and will forgive us our sins and purify us from all unrighteousness."* He wants to forgive us and He wants us to live with Him. Jesus loves us so much that He was willing to take your sins and my sins and place them upon Himself. He took our punishment on the cruel, cruel cross. All we need to do is say, "God I am sorry for my sin, forgive me. Help me live the life that will be pleasing to you."

God could have put a price on this living water that none of us could afford. It is worth much more than any of us have. But instead, He gives it freely to those who love Him. Heaven is the perfect place, and it is waiting for anyone who chooses to walk faithfully with the Lord.

I am looking forward to this place of no more death, mourning, crying or pain. I can't imagine what my first walk on the streets of gold will be like, as I gaze at the crystal sea, and marvel at all of the precious stones on the walls of that great city! And then to look upon my Savior who died for me….there is no other place I would rather be! It will make all my denials here on earth, the trials, problems, and pains, all worthwhile. Live for such a place. LIVE FOR ETERNITY.

Conclusion

I remember a trip that I took with my cousin and her husband, who was her fiancé at the time. We were going to a softball tournament in Indiana. As we were traveling along Route 74, we were driving on a newly constructed road. It was the smoothest road that I have ever been on. As we approached our next route, I jokingly said to them, "This is such a great road, let's just stay on it." I was obviously teasing, because I knew that if we stayed on this road we would end up far from our destination. The easy and smooth road doesn't always lead us to the place where we want to be. It is the same way in our spiritual lives. We could easily choose the easiest path, but we need to make sure that it will lead us to our destination, which is heaven.

Many Christians are not living out what they believe. They profess with their mouth to be a Christian, but their lifestyle sends another message. I believe that how we live our lives says a lot about what we truly believe. If we believe something strong enough it affects our behaviors. Look at the lives of the disciples. They believed Jesus was the Messiah, the Christ, and their lives showed their belief. They left their family, friends, jobs, and homes to follow Jesus. They were willing to follow, even though they knew that persecution and death might lie ahead of them. Their actions matched their beliefs.

In the same way, our actions match our beliefs.

Picture with me a husband who says, "I love my wife," yet he verbally and physically abuses her, he is unfaithful to her, and is totally unwilling to sacrifice anything to make his wife happy. Does he really love his wife? I say no way! These are just words. If he truly loved his wife, his actions would be different. He would stop yelling and beating her, he would be faithful to her alone, and he would be willing to reprioritize his life to make her happy. Our actions do match what we believe! If they don't, we don't believe in it strongly enough to change our behaviors.

There are many times that people claim their belief in Jesus as Lord, but I am skeptical that many hold that as a true conviction. We profess Christ, but live our lives however we see fit. We reject living our lives by the standards that Jesus set for us because Christ's ways are not the self gratifying ways—they are the self denying ways. Jesus says pick up your cross daily and follow me, which means to die to yourself each day. Kill your selfish worldly desires and live your life for Christ. It's not an easy thing to do. Can we say like the Apostle Paul in Acts 20:24, *"However, I consider my life worth nothing to me, if only I may finish the race and complete the task the Lord Jesus has given me—the task of testifying to the gospel of God's grace."* Give up your own desires, and run your race for Him.

You might say, "Why would I want to live a sacrificial life? No one else does!" You should want to do this because that is the life Jesus modeled for us and has called us to live. I stand amazed as I reflect on the sacrifices Jesus made. He was fully God—He was in a perfect place, full of glory that He deserves. However, He left all of that to come to earth and live among fallen humanity. Philippians 2 says, "He emptied himself". Jesus stripped out of His glory and dressed Himself in frail humanity, yet He did not commit one sin. He endured ridicule and persecution with love and forgiveness. Then He faced the cruel cross. He did that, not for Himself, but for you and me. He did it to give us eternal life.

That is why I want to live a sacrificial life—to please my Creator and Redeemer. When we live such a life, we can have confidence of what lies ahead. In 2 Timothy 4:7-8, Paul says as he comes to the end of this life, *"I have fought the good fight, I have finished the race, I have kept the faith. Now there is in store for me the crown of righteousness, which the Lord, the righteous Judge, will award to me on that day—and not only to me, but also to all who have longed for his appearing."* Paul stood at the end of his life, at the end of his race, not regretting how he lived his life. He was ready to meet his Savior.

How about you? Are you running the race that God has for you? The course is marked out—the rules are plainly set in His Word. When you run a race and you give it all you've got, what a great feeling it is when you cross the finish line. When we have faithfully finished running our race in this world, Jesus will welcome us at the finish line with open arms saying, "Well done my good and faithful servant. GOOD RACE!"

About The Author

Kurt Litwiller has been the head pastor at Boynton Mennonite Church in Hopedale, Illinois, since April of 2001. He graduated with a Master's of Divinity degree from Lincoln Christian Seminary in December of 2001. He also holds a Sports Management degree from Goshen College in Indiana (1995) and a Liberal Arts degree from Hesston College in Kansas (1993). He married his wife Janelle in the summer of 2008, and they enjoy impacting lives together for the kingdom of God in their little town of Hopedale.

References

[1] Matthew 7:14-15.

[2] Craig Brian Larson, "Strong to the Finish", Preaching Today, Tape No. 155.

[3] Matthew 5:28.

[4] Matthew 5:21-22.

[5] Tan, Paul Lee, *Encyclopedia of 7,700 Illustrations*, (Garland, Texas: Bible Communications, Inc.) 1996.

[6] Genesis 2:16-17; Genesis 3:2-3.

[7] Promise Keepers, "Go the Distance", conference (8-11-00). (preachingtoday.com)

[8] John 12:6.

[9] Luke 22:4-6.

[10] Matthew 14:25-31.

[11] "Parable of an Overcomer", Preachingtoday.com, Submitted by Bruce Shelly.

[12] Greg Asimakoupoulos, Naperville, Illinois; source: Bill Bright, "How to Be Filled with the Spirit" (Campus Crusade publication).   (preachingtoday.com)

[13] Matthew 22:16.

[14] Matthew 9:14.

[15] http://www.victorshepherd.on.ca/Sermons/seven.htm

[16] Ibid.

[17] John 1:29.

[18] Swindoll, Charles R. *Swindoll's Ultimate Book of Illustrations & Quotes* (Thomas Nelson Publishers, 1998), 162.

[19] http://familyofchrist.net/sermons/Sermons2007/discipleship_Aug2007/How%20Jesus%20Did%20Church-Discipleship2.pdf

[20] http://www.victorshepherd.on.ca/Sermons/seven.htm

[21] Ibid.

[22] http://docs.google.com/viewer?a=v&q=cache:4QoeXl3EB8IJ:www.hamptonbaptist.org/Sermons/01.27.08_LeavingthePastBehind_Matthew4.pdf+sermons+on+matthew+4:18-22+Alexander+the+Great&hl=en&gl=us&pid=bl&srcid=ADGEESiUXHgJa2v9EX0tRWSdt_RWC4yKn_kHb00lgCnWbIrmZWBM1_qXyPeKGi2sfXv0k-9UA6_2t-xidGaiZFbu6y69kLXWUTgnvr9Gc76NIPn6cP_Tt9fIn6ZdWwzHU5PhW43pW2O4&sig=AHIEtbQNu5mEY9xY7GNOH5dinpjr3_zBcw

[23] Exodus 24:7

[24] Alcorn, Randy. *Treasure Principle* (Multnomah Publishers, 1995), 25.

[25] Ibid., 76.

[26] "Tithing down 62% in the Past Year", Barna Research Online (5-19-03) (preachingtoday.com)

[27] Clara Null, Oklahoma City, Oklahoma, Christian Reader, "Lite Fare."

[28] Many argue that a tithe does not have to go to the church, that it can be used anywhere in God's kingdom. I believe that the tithe goes to the church. The people of Israel were told to bring in the whole tithe into my house (Temple). On top of bringing a tithe to the temple, the Israelites were suppose to care for strangers, welcome traveling preachers, look after the widows and orphans, feed the poor, etc.. I believe as Christians, we should bring the tithe to the church and also give generously to the work of God's kingdom in other ways. The tithe should be the minimum that we give, not the maximum.

[29] Matthew 5:28.

[30] Matthew 5:21-22.

[31] Bob Russell, "Take the Risk," Preaching Today, Tape No. 143.

[32] Haddon Robinson, author and Gordon-Conwell Seminary professor, Preaching Today #200.

[33]Alcorn, 44.

[34]Ibid., 53.

[35]Ibid., 13.

[36]Ibid., 17-18.

[37]http://www.ccminternational.org/English/who_said_that/jim%20elliot.htm

[38]Alcorn, 19.

[39]Gaylord, Goertsen in The Christian Leader (February 26, 1991). Christianity Today, Vol. 35, no. 7. (preachingtoday.com)

[40]Joke a Day Ministries Group; submitted by Keith Todd, www.sermonfodder.com (preachingtoday.com)

[41]Martyrs Mirror (Herald Press, Second English printing, 2004), 741-742.

[42]http://www.calpeacepower.org/0201/forgiveness.htm

[43]"Student Auctions off Virginity for Offers of More Than £2.5 Million," U.K. Daily Telegraph (01/12/09); submitted by Sam O'Neal, Geneva, Illinois (preachingtoday.com)

[44]Luke 22:42-44.

[45]1 Kings 11:4.

[46]Sherman L. Burford, Fairmont, West Virginia. Leadership, Vol. 17, no. 2. (preachingtoday.com)

[47]http://www.house.gov/cummings/speech/sp120400.htm; Submitted by Chuck Sackett, Lincoln, Illinois. (preachingtoday.com)

[48]Strive to Humor daily e-mail list (12-19-01); submitted by Doug Diehl, San Antonio, Texas. (preachingtoday.com)

[49]Gray, Alice Stories of the Heart. (Multnomah Books, 1996), "Object Lesson" by John MacArthur, 264.

[50]Gray, Alice Stories of the Heart. (Multnomah Books, 1996), "Really Winning" by Michael Broome, 28.

[51]John 23:34

[52]K.P. Yohannan, "Christ's Call".

[53]Bryan Chapell, The Wonder of It All (Crossway, 1999); quoted in Men of Integrity (January/February 2001) (preachingtoday.com)

[54]http://www.worshipmap.com/sermons/piper-names-rev21.html

[55]Ibid.

[56]Warren Keating, The Joyful Noiseletter (preachingtoday.com)

[57]John 19:30.

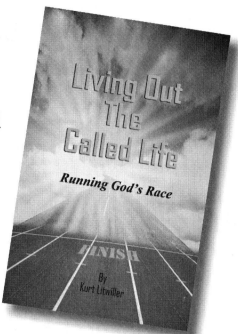

Need additional copies?

To order more copies of
Living Out The Called Life,
contact NewBookPublishing.com

☐ Order online at NewBookPublishing.com

☐ Call 877-311-5100 or

☐ Email Info@NewBookPublishing.com

Call for multiple copy discounts!

Reliance
Media

Another book by Kurt Litwiller:

New Covenant Living

Released to Live by the Spirit

God created us to have a relationship with Him, but unfortunately man sinned which separated us from God. Then God told Abraham that he was going to have a child, and in that way, He was going to call Abraham's descendants back into a relationship with Him. God gave His people, the Israelites, the law for them to enter into a covenant relationship with Him. Again and again, Israel could not hold up their end of the covenant and live according to God's Holy standards. Then, because of God's great love for us, He sent us His Son. Jesus came down to die upon the cross which ushered in a new covenant relationship between God and man. We now come to God through the new covenant of His blood. Read what the Apostle Paul meant when he said, "But if you are led by the Spirit, you are not under law."

To order copies of
New Covenant Living,
contact NewBookPublishing.com

❐ Order online at NewBookPublishing.com
❐ Call 877-311-5100 or
❐ Email Info@NewBookPublishing.com